Daniel

A closer look at the book that tells what will happen in the end times

by Kenneth Cox

649 East Chicago Road
Coldwater MI 49036
517-279-1304
www.remnantpublications.com

Cover Design by Penny Hall
Text Layout by Greg Solie – Altamont Graphics

ISBN 1-883012-37-6

Table of Contents

Study of Daniel

INSIDE THE STUDY OF DANIEL:

Introduction

Getting Acquainted

INSIDE THE INTRODUCTION:

Acknowledgements

How do you say thank you to so many people? If you are in debt deep enough to a person you become a partner. So with this book I am a debtor to so many that it has become a partnership of information. I am an evangelist, not a theologian; however, I have spent a lifetime studying the books of Daniel and Revelation. Desiring to understand the inspired messages of the prophet Daniel, I have read thousands of pages of commentaries, books, and articles on this intriguing book. As the years have come and gone, I have grown in my understanding, and am enthralled by the accuracy and depth of God's Word.

I would like to thank those whose books I have read and gathered information from for the writing of this book. I am indebted to Frank and Donna Sheffield for sharing the information from their research. It has been such a blessing studying the prophecies of this book together. Paul said, "And I urge you also, true companion, help these women who labored with me in the gospel" (Philippians 4:3). I will forever be indebted to the women who have labored with me in the gospel. This book would never have come to completion without the help of Diane Loer and Lindi McDougal. I owe much to the long hours they spent in layout and editing. Dona Klein has given her life to this ministry and has been an invaluable help in sentence construction and suggestions for the readability of this book. Maddy Couperus and Mabel Custer did much work in editing. To these, I am a debtor, and give my heartfelt thanks. It is my prayer, that as Daniel was given a vision concerning our day, this book will be a help in understanding where we are and where we are going.

—Kenneth Cox

Preface—Why Study Daniel?

Prophecy and miracles distinguish the Bible from any other book. If you take these two important parts out of Scripture all you have left is philosophy, making the Bible no different from any other writing. The book of Daniel is so broad in its prophecies that a person must either accept it as being inspired, or reject it for being fraudulent.

Many critics have said that Daniel could not have written the book of Daniel because he mentions too many things that happened after his lifetime. They try to place the writing of the book in the second century B.C. The problem with this approach is that many of Daniel's prophecies extend in time far beyond the second century B.C. In fact, they come clear down to the present time and onward to the Second Coming of Jesus Christ.

So, if the person writing the book of Daniel had lived in 200 B.C. he would still be prophesying about last day events. If he had lived during this time, he would not have been able to give the detailed descriptions that Daniel gave of the things that were happening in the sixth century B.C.

To the Christian, one of the most important points in establishing the credibility of Daniel's prophecies is that Jesus Christ accepted Daniel as inspired and quoted him in Matthew 24:15, "Therefore when you see the *'abomination of desolation'* , spoken of by Daniel the prophet, standing in the holy place (whoever reads, let him understand)." To the Christian believer this testimony should be convincing evidence.

Once you accept the book of Daniel as being inspired, all Scripture begins to fall into place. All the prophecies of Daniel are repeated in the book of Revelation and help us see clearly what is taking place today. The book of Daniel is a book of prophecy; whereas, the book of Revelation reveals what has been foretold. As you go through the chapters of Daniel, you will see the hand of God pointing out the destiny of nations. It will give you a solid foundation upon which to build your faith. As Daniel said to Nebuchadnezzar, "But there is a God in heaven who reveals secrets and He has made known … what will be in the latter days" (2:28).

Structure of Daniel

Chapter 1 Introduction
Explains how Daniel and his friends arrived in Babylon.

Chapters 2 and 7
These chapters deal with the same events.
Chapter 2 Illustrates using metals.
Chapter 7 Illustrates using beasts and gives more detail than chapter 2.

Chapters 3 and 6
These chapters are closely related.
Chapter 3 God's people refuse to worship the image.
Chapter 6 God's people show the results of the true worship of God.

Chapters 4 and 5
Both chapters deal with the fall of powers.
Chapter 4 The fall of the leader of Babylon.
Chapter 5 The system of Babylon falls.

Chapter 8
Further identifies the beasts of previous chapters.

Chapter 9
Deals with the seventy-week prophecy and expands on the subject of the 2,300 days mentioned in verse 8:14.

Chapters 10 through 12
Forms the last prophecy of the book of Daniel. This is God's final message to Daniel.

Middle East in Daniel's Day

T he Jordan River runs north from the Dead Sea to the Sea of Galilee and on to the country of Lebanon. From the southeast the river Euphrates makes its way into Lebanon. Much of Daniel's travel took place along these rivers. Because of the fertile soil, verdant vegetation and abundant water, this area was known as the Fertile Crescent. Most of this territory was controlled by the nation of Assyria.

King Ashurbonapal had grown old and his sons were weak leaders. In Babylon, his vice-regent Nebolpalazzar, saw his opportunity to take over the kingdom. In 612 B.C. he overthrew the Assyrian capital of Nineveh. The Babylonians became the masters of the Middle East. A group of Assyrians went up to the city of Carchemish to revolt against the Babylonian rule.

Nebolpalazzar was old and turned to his son, Nebuchadnezzar, to put down the revolt. While Nebuchadnezzar made his way up to Carchemish, the Pharaoh of Egypt decided to get involved in the battle. If he could overthrow Nebuchadnezzar, then Egypt would gain control of all the Middle East. Pharaoh-Necho passed through Israel on his way up to Carchemish. Israel's young king Josiah went out to stop him, and was killed in battle in the Valley of Megiddo. Nebuchadnezzar not only put down the revolt in Carchemish, but also defeated Pharaoh-Necho. While pursuing him back to Egypt, he decided to bring Israel under his dominion. As he subdued Israel, Nebuchadnezzar received word that his father had died. He immediately left for Babylon, but commanded his captain to bring back approximately fifty young men of royal blood to be trained in the courts of Babylon. Thus Daniel and his companions were carried off to Babylon (See the following map).

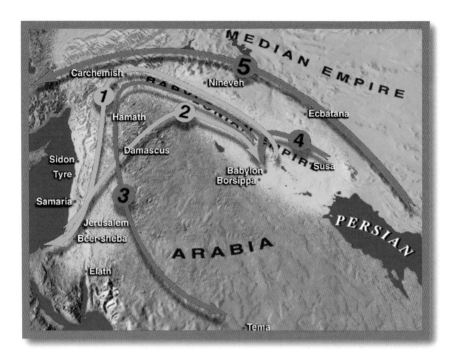

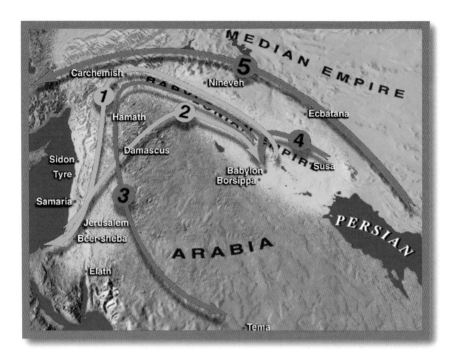 Nebuchadnezzar made three principal campaigns to Palestine:
1. In 605 B.C. taking captives, including Daniel.
2. In 597 B.C. taking Jehoiachin and others, including Ezekiel.
3. From 588–586 B.C. besieging and destroying Jerusalem and taking Zedekiah and thousands of other captives. For more on these campaigns, see 2 Kings 25; 2 Chronicles 36.

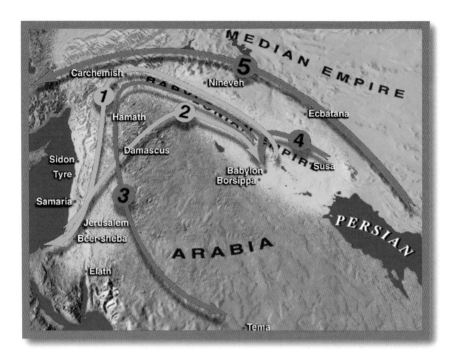 Nebuchadnezzar hurried home across the desert when his father died in 605 B.C., leaving captives to be brought home by the army via the longer route.

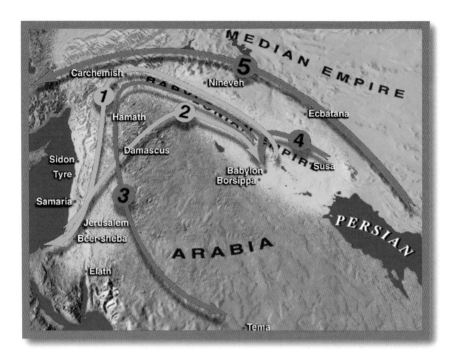 Nabonidus went to Tema, via Lebanon, (552 B.C.), placing Belshazzar in charge of Babylonia during his extended absence.

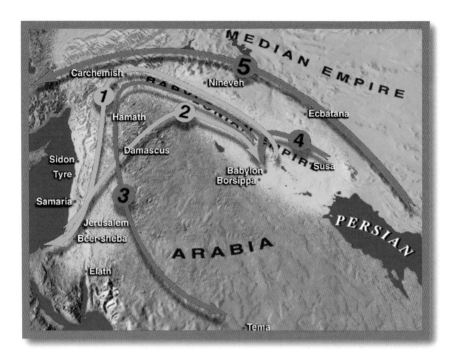 Cyrus' campaign against Babylon in 539 B.C.

 Cyrus' campaign against Media and Lydia in 550–547 B.C.

Daniel the Righteous

The Bible presents only two individuals as being without fault, other than Jesus Christ. They are Joseph and Daniel. Ezekiel, a contemporary of Daniel, referred to him as being righteous (Ezekiel 14:14).

Daniel was only eighteen years of age when he was brought to the king's court in Babylon. He stood without rival in physical strength and beauty, in mental vigor and literary attainment, and in spiritual power and insight. In all matters of wisdom and understanding, the king found Daniel ten times better than all the magicians and astrologers in his realm.

To mankind, Daniel is an example of what the power of God can accomplish in the life of an individual who is totally dedicated to serving the Lord. Daniel was true, noble and generous. While he was anxious to be at peace with all humanity, he would not permit any power to turn him aside from the path of duty. Even when serving in a pagan court where the circumstances were against what he believed, Daniel remained faithful.

Daniel held a high position in the courts of Babylon, yet served and honored God. He was neither proud nor self-sufficient. He felt the need of refreshing his soul with prayer, and 3 times each day found him in earnest supplication before God.

The prophecies Daniel received directly from God were given especially for these last days. The visions he saw by the banks of the Ulai, the Hiddekel (Hebrew name for the Tigris River), and the great rivers of Shinar, are now in the process of fulfillment. All the events foretold will soon come to pass. Because of Daniel's integrity and his dependence upon the Almighty, he was a man "greatly beloved" of heaven.

PERSONALITY PROFILE: DANIEL

Also Known As: Belteshazzar
Belteshazzar—Babylonian name means, "Bel Provides".
Daniel—Hebrew name means, "God is Judge".

Home: Judea. Most of his life was spent in Babylon.

Family: Nothing is told about his family except that he was of royal birth. Thus he would be from the tribe of Judah.

Occupation: Statesman, Prophet and Prime Minister of two nations (Babylonian and Persian Empires).

Special Interests: Prophecies concerning the Jewish people and their return to Jerusalem. Also the rise and fall of nations bringing man down to the "Time of the End".

Best Known Today As: The author of the book of Daniel.
"Daniel, go your way till the end; for you shall rest, and will arise to your inheritance at the end of days" (Daniel 12:13).

Tour of Daniel

Daniel's Captivity (1:1–21)
This chapter opens with Daniel and his friends being taken to Babylon. Don't miss their stand of faith and God's blessing.

Nebuchadnezzar's Dream (2:1–49)
With the touch of Omnipotence, God traces the future of the world. This chapter is the bedrock of understanding Bible prophecy.

Fiery Furnace (3:1–30)
One of the greatest examples of faith in the Scriptures.

Nebuchadnezzar's Conversion (4:1–37)
A dramatic display of power as God humbles Nebuchadnezzar, who then accepts His sovereignty.

The Fall Of Babylon (5:1–31)
Handwriting on the palace wall brings an end to Belshazzar's reign and his life.

Daniel In The Lions' Den (6:1–28)
Meet Darius the new king and observe Daniel's refusal to change his lifestyle in the face of death.

Four Great Beasts (7:1–28)
Daniel's dream continues to show the future of man, as God reveals in greater detail the events to take place in our day.

The Ram, the Goat and the Little Horn (8:1–12)

The vision continues to repeat and enlarge as the Lord shows in greater detail the events to take place.

The Vision of the 2,300 Days (8:13–19)

The angel Gabriel tells Daniel that this vision has to do with the Time of the End.

The Angel Gabriel Explains the Vision (9:1–27)

Daniel prays for understanding in verses 3–23 and the Lord sends Gabriel to make the vision clear.

View of the Great Conflict (10:1–21)

Daniel is given an opportunity to see the battle that is going on between the forces of good and evil.

King of the North and King of the South (11:1–45)

The hand of God writes out the conflict between these two powers, reaching from the days of Daniel to the end of time.

Time of the End (12:1–13)

There will be a time of trouble at the very end. Daniel is assured that the vision will be fulfilled as prophesied, and the righteous will be saved.

People You Will Meet in Daniel

Nebuchadnezzar the King of Babylon

The pompous king who ruled Babylon forty years and had a wonderful conversion.

Hananiah known as Shadrach

One of Daniel's three friends who was taken to Babylon. His Hebrew name meant, "The Lord is gracious". His Chaldean name meant, "Exalt Aku".

Mishael known as Meshach

One of the three Hebrew worthies taken to Babylon with Daniel. His Hebrew name meant, "Who is what the Lord is". His Chaldean name meant, "Who is what Aku is".

Azariah known as Abed-Nego

The third Hebrew worthy and one of the three you will meet at the Fiery Furnace. His Hebrew name meant, "The Lord is my helper". His Chaldean name meant, "The servant of Nebo".

Belshazzar the King of Babylon

Nebuchadnezzar's grandson who did not follow the Lord, and whose kingdom was taken away.

Darius the King of Medo-Persia

The compassionate king who honored Daniel.

Cyrus the King of Persia

Mentioned by God in the book of Isaiah a hundred years before he was born (Isaiah 45:1). Founder of the Persian Empire.

Places and People You Will Visit in Daniel

Babylon

See the "Closer Look" for 4:28–30.

Shinar

In Genesis 14:1, 9 Shinar seems to be the name of an area in Northern Mesopotamia called *SanhÉar*. The Shinar mentioned in Daniel is Babylonia, as in Genesis 11:2; Isaiah 11:11; Zechariah 5:11.

Chaldeans

An Aramaean tribe whose early settlement was in Lower Mesopotamia and who took over the rulership of Babylonia when Nabopolassar founded the Neo-Babylonian dynasty. In this book this term applies to a class of scholars in the Babylonian court who were the foremost astronomers of their day.

Soothsayers

The generally accepted meaning is "the deciders", or "the determiners (of destiny)". They thought they could determine the future from the position of the stars, by various arts of computation and divining.

Satraps

The governors of the provinces of ancient Persia.

Terms for Your Tour Explained

Day For A Year (In Bible Prophecy)

The day for a year principal has been recognized by Bible students down through the ages. Joachim, Abbot of Calabria, one of the great ecclesiastical figures of the twelfth century, applied the year/day principal to the 1,260-year period. "The woman, clothed with the sun, who signifies the church, remained hidden in the wilderness from the face of the serpent, twelve hundred and sixty days for the same number of years" (*Joachim of Floris, Concordantia*, Book 2, chapter 16, p. 12). Sir Isaac Newton used it in his book, *Observations Upon the Prophecies of Daniel* (pp. 127, 128). Moses Stuart said, "It is a singular fact that the great mass of interpreters in the English and the American world have, for many years, been wont to understand the days designated in Daniel and in the Apocalypse, as the representatives of symbols of years. I have found it difficult to trace the origin of this general, I might say almost universal, custom" (*Hints on the Interpretation of Prophecy*, p. 74). The supporters of a day for a year in Bible prophecy have been theologians such as Augustine, Tichonius, Andreas, Bebe, Ambrosius, Ansbertus, Berengaud, besides the leading modern expositors. But the most convincing fact is that the prophecies have been fulfilled based on this principle. You will find this to be true with the prophecies of Daniel 7; 9 and Revelation 11; 12; 13.

Dominion Taken Away

The territory of Babylon was made subject to Persia, yet the subjects of Babylon were allowed to live on. Similarly, when Macedonia conquered Persia and when Rome conquered Macedonia, the inhabitants of the conquered countries were not destroyed.

Eyes

Generally taken to be a symbol of intelligence. In contrast with the Barbarians, who were largely illiterate, the power represented by the "Little Horn" was noted for its intelligence, its insight and its foresight.

Four Winds

Frequently in Scripture the "four winds" represent the four directions of the compass (See 8:8; 11:4; Jeremiah 49:36; Zechariah 2:6; 6:5; Mark 13:27). This can represent political or warlike activity in various parts of the earth. Probably the closest parallel is found in Daniel 7:2 and Revelation 7:1, where they appear to be the forces of strife out of which great nations arise.

Lion With Eagle's Wings

A lion is noted for its strength; whereas, the eagle is famous for its power and the range of its flight. Nebuchadnezzar's power was felt not only in Babylon but from the Mediterranean to the Persian Gulf, and from Asia Minor to Egypt. Thus it is fitting, to represent the spread of Babylon's power, that the lion should be provided with eagle's wings. (Lamentations 4:19; Habakkuk 1:6–8.)

Times (As used in Daniel 4:16)

The majority of both past and present explanations of the Aramaic word *iddan*, are defined as "time" (See also verses 23, 25, 32; 7:25). The Hebrew and Chaldee Dictionary defines it as "A set time, technically, a year; time".

Was Slain

This represents the end of the system, or organization, symbolized by the horn. Paul refers to the same power as the "man of sin" and the "son of perdition". He speaks of its destruction at the Second Coming of Christ. (2 Thessalonians 2:3–8; Revelation 19:19–21.)

Wind

Symbolically denotes activity or energy of some form, to be determined by the context. The "winds" of Daniel, which strove upon the great sea, causing four beasts—or empires—to emerge, represented diplomatic movements , warlike, political, or otherwise, that were to shape history.

Road Map to Using This Book

I have tried to keep this book brief, clear and easy to understand. All the Scripture references refer to the book of Daniel unless otherwise stated. The Bible translation used is the New King James Version.

Where Do I Start?

The best way to get the most out of this book is:

1. Read the entire chapter first.
2. Go back and read the texts along with the explanation.

NOTE: Where an explanation is given, an icon will be shown along with the texts that are being explained. If you will follow the explanations in order, it will help clarify many of the points in question.

There is a chart listing all the prophecies of Daniel at the end of chapter 7. They are placed on a time-line showing how the prophecies have been fulfilled and where we are in the stream of time. Refer to this chart as you read and study.

It is my hope that this book will help you see the unerring accuracy of God's Word, and the wonderful love and care of God for mankind. Above all else, it is my prayer that you will be led to accept Jesus Christ as your Savior.

Road Signs for Your Tour

I have used four icons to identify the explanations.

Consider This

Certain texts offer a deeper insight into God's Word. In these cases I used this icon with the texts saying, **"Consider This."**

Closer Look

As history or events open up the understanding of a particular Scripture, this icon is used with the statement, **"Closer Look."**

Key to Prophecy

There are principles in understanding Bible prophecy that are consistent throughout Scripture. In these cases this icon is used with the phrase, **"Key to Prophecy."**

Faith Builders

Daniel and his friends were men of great faith. I have expanded on six incidents in the book of Daniel which demonstrate this. These are entitled, **"Faith Builders."** Whatever lessons we can learn from these men to increase our faith will help us in our walk with the Lord. "For without faith it is impossible to please God" (Hebrews 11:6).

Chapter 1

Daniel's Captivity

INSIDE THIS CHAPTER:

1:1, 2 Removal of the Articles from the House of God

1. In the third year of the reign of Jehoiakim king of Judah, Nebuchadnezzar king of Babylon came to Jerusalem and besieged it. 2. And the Lord gave Jehoiakim king of Judah into his hand, with some of the articles of the house of God, which he carried into the land of Shinar to the house of his god; and he brought the articles into the treasure house of his god.

1:1, 2 TREASURE LOST

Consider This

At this time the temple was the treasure house for most nations. The rulers believed that the safest place for their wealth was in their temples because their gods were greatly revered. No doubt Nebuchadnezzar carried off the finest and most valuable temple vessels. Since they were made of gold, this amounted to millions of dollars.

1:3–7 The Deportation of Youth to Babylon

3. Then the King instructed Ashpenaz, the master of his eunuchs, to bring some of the children of Israel and some of the king's descendants and some of the nobles, 4. young men in whom there was no blemish, but good-looking, gifted in all wisdom, possessing knowledge and quick to understand, who had ability to serve in the king's palace, and whom they might teach the language and literature of the Chaldeans. 5. And the king appointed for them a daily provision of the king's delicacies and of the wine which he drank, and three years of training for them, so that at the end of that time they might serve before the king. 6. Now from among those of the sons of Judah were Daniel, Hananiah, Mishael, and Azariah. 7. To them the chief of the eunuchs gave names: he gave Daniel the name Belteshazzar; to Hananiah, Shadrach; to Mishael, Meshach; and to Azariah, Abed-Nego.

1:3–7 A WORLD OF DIFFERENCE

Consider This

In choosing the young men, the king asked for the three things the world considers most important: good looks, intelligence and great social graces. But God places spiritual characteristics above these three. Daniel and his friends had all four.

1:3–7 BRAINWASHING TECHNIQUES

Consider This

The idea of brainwashing is not new to our age. Nebuchadnezzar understood if these young men were going to serve in his court, a complete change would be required. The king set in action the steps that would bring about the needed change.

Nebuchadnezzar's Brainwashing Techniques

Chaldean Education (Daniel 1:4)

To teach them the language and literature of the Chaldeans would help them forget the heritage and beliefs they had been taught as children. These were young men who were still impressionable and now was the time to make the change. A good daily dose of educated paganism could wipe out the past.

A Sense of Obligation (Daniel 1:5)

What a unique privilege to eat food from the king's table and drink the wine that was served to the king. They never had it like this at home. Look at all the king was doing for them. It would not be hard to get used to this kind of life. Nebuchadnezzar really wasn't such a bad fellow after all.

Change Their Heritage (Daniel 1:7)

Their Hebrew names were a constant reminder that they had been dedicated to God by their parents. The Babylonian names would help them forget about the God of their fathers and turn them to the worship of the gods after which they were now named (See "People You Will Meet in Daniel" p. 16 for an explanation of these name changes).

Give Up Their Belief (Daniel 1:8)

Before being taken captive, Daniel, as well as all the Hebrew young men who had been carried to Babylon, had been taught that they were not to eat unclean meats (Leviticus 11). Also, it was forbidden to eat food that had been offered to a pagan god (Deuteronomy 7). The individual who used fermented wine was considered unwise (Proverbs 20:1). To participate in eating and drinking at the king's table would require giving up their belief in the Word of God. In order for the brainwashing process to work this step was absolutely necessary.

Change of Lifestyle (Daniel 1:10)

Only when a person has changed the way he lives has the brainwashing technique worked. Twice in Scripture we are told of efforts made to cause Daniel to change his lifestyle. Here he was being asked to change his eating habits. In chapter 6 he was asked to stop praying to his God each day.

These methods were so effective that out of approximately fifty to seventy young men who were taken to Babylon, only four survived the ordeal and kept their faith.

1:8–16 The Faithfulness of Daniel in Babylon

8. But Daniel purposed in his heart that he would not defile himself with the portion of the king's delicacies, nor with the wine which he drank; therefore he requested of the chief of the eunuchs that he might not defile himself. 9. Now God had brought Daniel in the favor and good will of the chief of the eunuchs. 10. And the chief of the eunuchs said to Daniel, "I fear my lord the king, who has appointed your food and drink. For why should he see your faces looking worse than the young men who are your age? Then you would endanger my head before the king." 11. So Daniel said to the steward whom the chief of the eunuchs had set over Daniel, Hananiah, Mishael, and Azariah, 12. "Please test your servants for ten days, and let them give us vegetables to eat and water to drink. 13. "Then let our countenances be examined before you, and the countenances of the young men who eat the portion of the king's delicacies: and as you see fit, so deal with your servants." 14. So he consented with them in this matter and tested them ten days. 15. And at the end of ten days their countenance appeared better and fatter in flesh than all the young men who ate the portion of the king's delicacies. 16. Thus the steward took away their portion of delicacies and the wine that they were to drink, and gave them vegetables.

#1 Faith Builder

Faith Builders   **Next Faith Builder   #2 Chapter 2:14–23**

1:8–16 UNCOMPROMISING LIFE

There are situations in the life of Daniel which give us indications of how he built his faith. Hebrews 11:6 says, without faith you cannot please God. The six examples in this book of how he built his faith are needed in today's hectic society.

Daniel was willing to receive a Babylonian education and to have his name changed, but there were two areas where he refused to compromise. To give in on these points would affect his faith in God:

1) Faith must be built on Scripture. The Word of God must be accepted as inspired by God, "… for doctrine, for reproof, for correction and for instruction in righteousness" (2 Timothy 3:16). This gave Daniel a firm foundation.

2) Once you have established your belief in God, your witness must be consistent with your belief, which determines your lifestyle. Daniel knew he could not sacrifice his lifestyle and keep his belief; therefore, he chose not to eat the food or drink the wine from the king's table. Men in Scripture, like Daniel, who stood true to what the Scripture taught had this testimony, "that they pleased God".

1:17–21 God Honors Daniel and His Companions

17. As for these four young men, God gave them knowledge and skill in all literature and wisdom: and Daniel had understanding in all visions and dreams. 18. Now at the end of the days, when the king had said that they should be brought in, the chief of the eunuchs brought them in before Nebuchadnezzar. 19. Then the king interviewed them, and among them all none was found like Daniel, Hananiah, Mishael, and Azariah; therefore they served before the king. 20. And in all matters of wisdom and understanding about which the king examined them, he found them ten times better than all the magicians and astrologers who were in all his realm. 21. Thus Daniel continued until the first year of King Cyrus.

1:17–21 FAITH REWARDED

Consider This

God, "… is a rewarder of those who diligently seek Him" (Hebrews 11:6). Daniel, Hananiah, Mishael and Azariah had sought Him in their daily lives and God honored their faith. Two gifts of the Holy Spirit, wisdom and knowledge, had been abundantly given to these worthy young men.

Chapter 2

Nebuchadnezzar's Dream

INSIDE THIS CHAPTER:

2:1–3 Nebuchadnezzar's Dream

1. Now in the second year of Nebuchadnezzar's reign, Nebuchadnezzar had dreams; and his spirit was so troubled that his sleep left him. 2. Then the king gave the command to call the magicians, and astrologers, the sorcerers, and the Chaldeans to tell the king his dreams. So they came and stood before the king. 3. And the king said to them, "I have had a dream, and my spirit is anxious to know the dream."

2:1–3 DREAM SPECIALIST

Consider This

Dreams were considered omens of events that would happen in future life; therefore, great effort was put forth to understand everything seen in a dream. The magicians, astrologers and sorcerers were experts in interpreting dreams. Archeologists have found whole libraries of clay tablets dedicated to the study of dreams. God brought Daniel to the forefront by giving the king a dream he could not recall. This dream had a profound impression on him.

2:4–11 Wise Men's Predicament

4. Then the Chaldeans spoke to the king in Aramaic, "O king, live forever! tell your servants the dream, and we will give the interpretation," 5. But the king answered and said to the Chaldeans, "My decision is firm: if you do not make known the dream to me, and its interpretation, you shall be cut in pieces, and your houses shall be made an ash heap. 6. "However, if you tell the dream and its interpretation, you shall receive from me gifts, rewards, and great honor. Therefore tell me the dream and its interpretation." 7. They answered again and said, "Let the king tell his servants the dream, and we will give its interpretation." 8. The king answered and said, "I know for certain that you would gain time, because you see that my decision is firm: 9. if you do not make known the dream to me, there is only one decree for you!

For you have agreed to speak lying and corrupt words before me till the time has changed. Therefore tell me the dream, and I shall know that you can give me its interpretation." 10. The Chaldeans answered the king, and said, "There is not a man on earth who can tell the king's matter; therefore no king, lord, or ruler has ever asked such things of any magician, astrologer, or Chaldean. 11. "It is a difficult thing that the king requires, and there is no other who can tell it to the king except the gods, whose dwelling is not with flesh."

2:4–11 WISE MEN'S PREDICAMENT

The king's wise men were not only asked to interpret the dream, but to tell the king what he had seen in the dream. They said this was impossible for any man to accomplish.

Consider This

2:12–15 The King's Death Decree

12. For this reason the king was angry and very furious, and gave a command to destroy all the wise men of Babylon. 13. So the decree went out, and they began killing the wise men; and they sought Daniel and his companions, to kill them. 14. Then with counsel and wisdom Daniel answered Arioch, the captain of the king's guard, who had gone out to kill the wise men of Babylon; 15. He answered and said to Arioch the king's captain, "Why is the decree from the king so urgent?" Then Arioch made the decision known to Daniel.

2:12–15 THE KING'S DEATH DECREE

Daniel and his companions were young men of approximately twenty years of age. They were considered novices, so when the king called in all his wise men they were not included. When the king gave the command to destroy the wise men; however, they were included.

Consider This

2:16–23 God Reveals the Dream

16. So Daniel went in and asked the king to give him time, that he might tell the king the interpretation. 17. Then Daniel went to his house, and made the decision known to Hananiah, Mishael, and Azariah, his companions, 18. That they might seek mercies from the God of heaven concerning this secret, so that Daniel and his companions might not perish with the rest of the wise men of Babylon. 19. Then the secret was revealed to Daniel in a night vision. So Daniel blessed the God of heaven. 20. Daniel answered and said: "Blessed be the name of God forever and ever, for wisdom and might are His. 21. And He changes the times and the seasons; He removes kings and raises up kings; He gives wisdom to the wise and knowledge to those who have understanding. 22. He reveals deep and secret things; He knows what is in the darkness, and light dwells with Him. 23. I thank You and praise You, O God of my fathers; You have given me wisdom and might, and have now made known to me what we asked of You, for You have made known to us the king's demand."

Faith Builders   **Next Faith Builder**   **#3 Chapter 3:16–18**

2:16–23 PRAYER AND PRAISE

There are situations in the life of Daniel which give us indications of how he built his faith. Hebrews 11:6 says, "Without faith you cannot please God". The six examples in this book of how he built his faith are needed in today's hectic society.

In the trial of his faith, Daniel used two of the greatest resources in the Christian life: prayer and praise. When crises arise, as they do in everyone's life, go to the Lord in prayer. As one writer said, "Prayer is the key in the hand of faith that unlocks heaven's storehouse."

"Now faith is the substance of things hoped for, the evidence of things not seen" (Hebrews 11:1). Daniel and his friends had not seen the dream that Nebuchadnezzar had, yet they believed God would answer their prayers. In faith they petitioned heaven to reveal the dream.

So often God answers our prayers and we do not think, or take the time, to praise Him for His goodness.

The hour was urgent. Men had already died. But Daniel took time to thank the Lord for answering his prayer. Praise is the highest form of expression and keeps us from becoming self-centered. It expresses our faith in the Almighty.

2:24–27 Daniel Goes Before the King

24. Therefore Daniel went to Arioch, whom the king had appointed to destroy the wise men of Babylon. He went and said thus to him: "Do not destroy the wise men of Babylon; take me before the king, and I will tell the king the interpretation," 25. Then Arioch quickly brought Daniel before the king, and said thus to him, "I have found a man of the captives of Judah, who will make known to the king the interpretation." 26. The King answered and said to Daniel, whose name was Belteshazzar, "Are you able to make known to me the dream which I have seen, and its interpretation?" 27. Daniel answered in the presence of the king, and said, "The secret which the king has demanded, the wise men, the astrologers, the magicians, and the soothsayers cannot declare to the king.

2:28–30 Daniel Tells the Dream

28. But there is a God in heaven who reveals secrets, and He has made known to King Nebuchadnezzar what will be in the latter days. Your dream, and the visions of your head upon your bed, were these; 29. "As for you, O king, thoughts came to your mind while on your bed, about what would come to pass after this; and He who reveals secrets has made known to you what will be. 30. But as for me, this secret has not been revealed to me because I have more wisdom than anyone living, but for our sakes who make known the interpretation to the king, and that you may know the thoughts of your heart.

2:28 TIME OF THE END

Closer Look

Special attention should be given to the fact that this vision Nebuchadnezzar received was concerning the latter days or "Time of the End."

2:31–35 The Great Image

31. "You, O King, were watching; and behold a great image! This great image, whose splendor was excellent, stood before you; and its form was awesome. 32. "This image's head was of fine gold, its chest and arms of silver, its belly and thighs of bronze, 33. "its legs of iron, its feet partly of iron and partly of clay. 34. "You

watched while a stone was cut out without hands, which struck the image on its feet of iron and clay, and broke them in pieces. 35. "Then the iron, the clay, the bronze, the silver, and the gold were crushed together, and became like chaff from the summer threshing floors; the wind carried them away so that no trace of them was found. And the stone that struck the image became a great mountain and filled the whole earth.

2:36, 37 Daniel Interprets the Dream

36. "This is the dream. Now we will tell the interpretation of it before the king. 37. "You, O king, are a king of kings. For the God of heaven has given you a kingdom, power, strength, and glory;

2:38 Head of Gold

38. "And wherever the children of men dwell, or the beasts of the field and the birds of the heaven, He has given them into your hand, and has made you ruler over them all—you are this head of gold.

2:38 BABYLON 605 B.C.

Closer Look

Nebuchadnezzar ruled forty of the seventy years Babylon existed. This is the reason God said "You are this head of gold." Historians referred to Babylon as the golden kingdom. It was the first kingdom in the vision.

2:39 Kingdoms of Silver and Bronze

39. "But after you shall arise another kingdom inferior to yours; then another, a third kingdom of bronze, which shall rule over all the earth.

2:39A MEDO-PERSIA 539 B.C.

Closer Look

Just as silver is inferior to gold, so the next kingdom would be inferior to Babylon. Babylon was overthrown by Medo-Persia under the leadership of Cyrus and fell in 539 B.C. God mentioned Cyrus by name a hundred years before he was born, and also described how he would overthrow the city of Babylon (Isaiah 45:1). This dramatic episode is related in Daniel chapter 5.

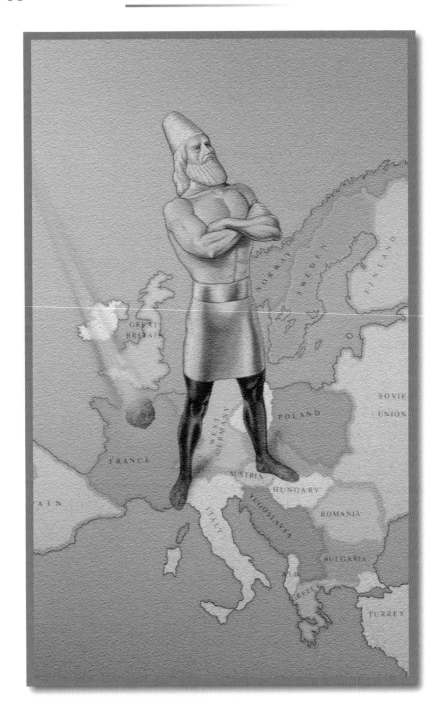

2:39B GREECE 331 B.C.

Closer Look

The third kingdom to come on the scene of existence was Greece. It, "… shall rule over all the earth" (2:39), meaning Greece would conquer all the nations of the earth. Alexander the Great, with forty-thousand men, faced Darius, whose army numbered one million, on the plains of Arbela. Implementing a new type of warfare, Alexander won the battle. The Bible stated that Greece would overthrow Medo-Persia. (8:1–8, 20, 21.)

2:40 Kingdom of Iron

40. "And the fourth kingdom shall be as strong as iron, inasmuch as iron breaks in pieces and shatters all things; and like iron that crushes, that kingdom will break in pieces and crush all the others.

2:40 PAGAN ROME 168 B.C.

Closer Look

Rome defeated Greece and ruled longer than any other power. This power controlled the world from 168 B.C. until A.D. 476. Historians refer to this kingdom as the "iron monarchy" (Source: Edward Gibbon, *The History of the Decline and Fall of the Roman Empire*). All that has been reconstructed of Roman history confirms this description. Rome won her territory by the force or the fear of armed might. She first intervened in international affairs in a struggle for her life against Carthage, and was drawn into war after war. She crushed one opponent after another and finally became the aggressive and able conqueror of the Mediterranean World and Western Europe. At the beginning of the Christian Era, and a little later, the iron might of the Roman legions stood in back of the Pax Romana—the Roman peace. At that time Rome was the largest and strongest empire the world had seen. Jesus was born during this reign.

2:41–43 Iron Mixed With Ceramic Clay

41. "Whereas you saw the feet and toes, partly of potter's clay and partly of iron, the kingdom shall be divided; yet the strength of the iron shall be in it, just as you saw the iron mixed with ceramic clay. 42. "And as the toes of the feet were partly of iron and partly of clay, so the kingdom shall be partly strong and partly fragile. 43. "As you saw iron mixed with ceramic clay, they will mingle with the seed of men, but they will not adhere to one another, just as iron does not mix with clay.

2:41–43A KINGDOM DIVIDED A.D. 476

Closer Look

One of the great phenomena of history took place when masses of people moved at once. They were called Goths or Barbarians. They began invading the Roman Empire, breaking it to pieces in A.D. 476. These Germanic people became the nations of Western Europe today:

Anglo-Saxons	England
Franks	France
Burgundians	Switzerland
Visigoths	Spain
Alamanni	Germany
Suevi	Portugal
Lombards	Italy
Heruli	Destroyed (A.D. 493)
Vandals	Destroyed (A.D. 534)
Ostrogoths	Destroyed (A.D. 538)

2:41–43B IRON MIXED WITH CERAMIC CLAY

Closer Look

"… They (the divided kingdoms) shall mingle with the seed of men" (2:43), refers to royal intermarriages. The word for man here is *enash*, "mankind." "Seed" here means descendants. At one time nearly all the European heads of state intermarried in an attempt to unify Europe. Even this could not prove the prophecy wrong: "… but they (the nations of Europe) will not adhere one to another" (2:43). Throughout history Satan has made at least seven attempts to prove this prophecy wrong. Charlemagne, Charles V, Louis XIV, Napoleon, Kaiser Wilhelm, Hitler and Mussolini all set out to unite Europe. A united Europe meant control of the world. All such plans have failed just as the Bible predicted. Some world powers have been weak, others strong—like the mixture of iron and clay.

Daniel's prophecy has stood and will stand the test of time. Today it carries special meaning because the dream was to show Nebuchadnezzar what was to take place in the latter days.

A careful study of the prophecies of Daniel and Revelation reveals that the ten kings of Daniel 2 are the same ten kings as those in Revelation 17, "… which have received no kingdom as yet" (Revelation 17:12). A study of Revelation 17 further reveals that, "as yet" refers to an exact time period. The Bible makes it clear that the ten kings have received, "no kingdom (singular) as yet". This doesn't say they haven't received their kingdoms (plural). These nations have been kingdoms since the breakup of the Roman Empire. (See "Closer Look" 2:41–43A.) They have not, "as yet" spoken with, "one mind" as referred to in Revelation 17:13. These nations will receive power from, or have some kind of an alliance with, the "beast", during a short period of time referred to as "one hour", just before the Second Coming of Jesus. The identity of this "beast" power will be examined in detail in subsequent chapters. During this, "one hour" period, "These (the nations of Europe) have one mind, and shall give their power and strength unto the beast" (Revelation 17:13).

Strong movements are taking place in Western Europe to bring together the ten toes, not as one kingdom, but working together to accomplish one objective. In 1992 under the Masstricht Treaty, the European Economic Community (created with the signature of the Treaty of Rome on March 25, 1957) emerged as the strongest economic trading block in the world. Today it directly involves fifteen nations with 400 million consumers. This is the first time since the Holy Roman Empire that Europe has been in a position to speak with one voice.

A poster circulated by the Council of Europe, one of the three main divisions of the European Economic Community, pictures the tower of Babel as its logo and the phrase, "Many Tongues, One Voice", as its motto. "The poster is a combination of a fifteenth century drawing of the tower of Babel, with the impression of a modern crane, illustrating that the Common Market alliance in 1992 will complete the building of a one-world order whose top will reach to Heaven. The twelve stars represent the 1990 membership of the Common Market". (*Europe is Rising!*, Oklahoma City, OK: Hearthstone Publishing, 1990, Inside cover.)

Earth's population is heading for a final showdown between the Power of Heaven and the powers of earth. God says the nations of Europe will not bond in a lasting union: "… they shall not cleave one to another" (2:43). Earthly powers say that those nations will once again be many tongues with one voice and are determined to have a complete political and economic union of Europe. "West Europeans mostly welcome the plans for monetary and political union". (*Time* Magazine, December 9, 1991).

The role the ten kings have assumed in recent years has placed the world on a collision course with the words of Daniel 2:43, "… they shall not cleave one to another." God says, "You won't," and the world says, "We will." It seems obvious that a confrontation between the Power of Heaven and the powers of earth will soon take place.

2:44, 45 Days of These Kings

44. "And in the days of these kings the God of heaven will set up a kingdom which shall never be destroyed; and the kingdom shall not be left to other people; it shall break in pieces and consume all these kingdoms and it shall stand forever. 45. Inasmuch as you saw that the stone was cut out of the mountain without hands, and that it broke in pieces the iron, the bronze, the clay, the silver, and the gold—the great God has made known to the king what will come to pass after this. The dream is certain, and its interpretation is sure."

2:44, 45 DAYS OF THESE KINGS

Closer Look

God told Nebuchadnezzar in his dream what was to happen in the latter days. As we have seen from Scripture the feet and toes were made up of iron and clay, showing that the fragments of the Roman Empire would be present in the "… days of these kings" (2:44). Developments in Western Europe to bring about unification of these kings that divided the Roman Empire, is indication of the nearness of Christ's return. Daniel has made it clear that just as sure as there was a Babylon, Medo-Persia, Greece, Rome and divided kingdom, the God of heaven will set up His kingdom that will last forever. The stone cut without human hands represents the literal Second Coming of Christ when all earthly power in opposition to Him will be demolished. As we see the events unfolding, we need to make sure we are citizens of the Heavenly Kingdom (A more detailed look is given in Revelation 17:12–14).

2:46–49 Nebuchadnezzar Promotes Daniel

46. Then King Nebuchadnezzar fell on his face, prostrate before Daniel, and commanded that they should present an offering and incense to him. 47. The king answered Daniel, and said, "Truly your God is the God of gods, the Lord of kings, and a revealer of secrets, since you could reveal this secret." 48. Then the king promoted Daniel and gave him many gifts; and he made him ruler over the whole province of Babylon, and chief administrator over all the wise men of Babylon. 49. Also, Daniel petitioned the king, and he set Shadrach, Meshach, and Abed-Nego over the affairs of the province of Babylon; but Daniel sat in the gate of the king.

Chapter 3

Fiery Furnace

INSIDE THIS CHAPTER:

3:1–7 Nebuchadnezzar's Golden Image

1. Nebuchadnezzar the king made an image of gold, whose height was sixty cubits and its width six cubits. He set it up in the plain of Dura, in the province of Babylon. 2. And King Nebuchadnezzar sent word to gather together the satraps, the administrators, the governors, the counselors, the treasurers, the judges, the magistrates, and all the officials of the provinces, to come to the dedication of the image which King Nebuchadnezzar had set up. 3. So the satraps, the administrators, the governors, the counselors, the treasurers, the judges, the magistrates, and all the officials of the provinces gathered together for the dedication of the image that King Nebuchadnezzar had set up; and they stood before the image that Nebuchadnezzar had set up. 4. Then a herald cried aloud; "To you it is commanded, O peoples, nations, and languages, 5. "That at the time you hear the sound of the horn, flute, harp, lyre, and psaltery, in symphony with all kinds of music, you shall fall down and worship the gold image that King Nebuchadnezzar has set up; 6. "and whoever does not fall down and worship shall be cast immediately into the midst of a burning fiery furnace." 7. So at that time, when all the people heard the sound of the horn, flute, harp, and lyre, in symphony with all kinds of music, all the people, nations, and languages fell down and worshiped the gold image which King Nebuchadnezzar had set up.

3:8–12 Shadrach, Meshach and Abed-Nego Refuse to Worship

8. Therefore at that time certain Chaldeans came forward and accused the Jews. 9. They spoke and said to King Nebuchadnezzar, "O king, live forever! 10. "You, O king, have made a decree that everyone who hears the sound of the horn, flute, harp, lyre, and psaltery, in symphony with all kinds of music, shall fall down and worship the gold image. 11. "and whoever does not fall down and worship shall be cast into the midst of a burning fiery furnace. 12. "There are certain Jews whom you have set over the affairs of the province of Babylon: Shadrach, Meshach, and Abed-Nego; these men, O king, have not paid due regard to you. They do not serve your gods or worship the gold image which you have set up."

3:13–18 Three Hebrew Worthies Trust God

13. Then Nebuchadnezzar, in rage and fury, gave the command to bring Shadrach, Meshach, and Abed-Nego. So they brought these men before the king. 14. Nebuchadnezzar spoke, saying to them, "Is it true Shadrach, Meshach, and Abed-Nego, that you do not serve my gods or worship the gold image which I have set up? 15. "Now if you are ready at the time you hear the sound of the horn, flute, harp, lyre, and psaltery, in symphony with all kinds of music, and you fall down and worship the image which I have made, good! But if you do not worship, you shall be cast immediately into the midst of a burning fiery furnace. And who is the god who will deliver you from my hands?" 16. Shadrach, Meshach, and Abed-Nego answered and said to the king, "O Nebuchadnezzar, we have no need to answer you in this matter. 17. "If that is the case, our God whom we serve is able to deliver us from the burning fiery furnace, and He will deliver us from your hand, O king. 18. "But if not, let it be known to you, O king, that we do not serve your gods, nor will we worship the gold image which you have set up."

Faith Builders   **Next Faith Builder**   **#4 Chapter 6:10, 11**

3 : 1 3 – 1 8
COMPLETE TRUST

There are situations in the life of Daniel which give us indications of how he built his faith. Hebrews 11:6 says, "Without faith you cannot please God." The six examples in this book of how he built his faith are needed in today's hectic society.

It takes two words to describe faith. We sometimes say, "that is his faith" meaning his or her belief. Belief is part of faith, but by itself it is not enough. To have what the Scriptures define as faith, you must have trust as well as belief. It is here that Shadrach, Meshach and Abed-Nego showed real faith. They told the king their God was able to deliver them, but if He did not, they would still trust Him and not worship

3:19–24 God Protects Shadrach, Meshach and Abed-Nego

19. Then Nebuchadnezzar was full of fury, and the expression on his face changed toward Shadrach, Meshach, and Abed-Nego. Therefore, he spoke and commanded that they heat the furnace seven times more than it was usually heated. 20. And he commanded certain mighty men of valor who were in his army to bind Shadrach, Meshach, and Abed-Nego, and cast them into the burning fiery furnace. 21. Then these men were bound in their coats, their trousers, their turbans, and their other garments, and were cast into the midst of the burning fiery furnace. 22. Therefore, because the king's command was urgent, and the furnace exceedingly hot, the flame of the fire killed those men who took up Shadrach, Meshach, and Abed-Nego. 23. And these three men, Shadrach, Meshach, and Abed-Nego fell down bound into the

midst of the burning fiery furnace. 24. Then King Nebuchadnezzar was astonished; and he rose in haste and spoke, saying to his counselors, "Did we not cast three men bound in the midst of the fire?" They answered and said to the king, "True, O king."

3:25 Son of God

25. "Look!" he answered, "I see four men loose, walking in the midst of the fire; and they are not hurt, and the form of the fourth is like the Son of God."

3:25 SON OF GOD

Consider This

Some commentators believe that the term "Son of God" refers to an angel. Here in the Aramaic, the word used for God can be interpreted as the true God. Jesus said, "Before Abraham was I Am" (John 8:56–59). "And now, O Father, glorify Me together with Yourself, with the glory which I had with you before the world was" (John 17:5). John the Baptist said Jesus existed before him (John 1:29, 30). Therefore it is not beyond the realm of possibility for Jesus to appear to comfort and encourage these three men. Without a doubt, this experience had a profound impression on Nebuchadnezzar and later contributed to his conversion in chapter 4.

Where was Daniel at this time? The image was erected on the plain of Dura which was located in the province of Babylon. 2:49 says the king set Shadrach, Meshach and Abed-Nego over the affairs of the province of Babylon, but Daniel, "... sat in the gate of the king" (2:49). The Hebrew and Chaldee Dictionary defines "Gate" as, "a door; impl. a palace:-gate mouth." The "gate" held great importance in ancient oriental cities (See Deuteronomy 21:19; 22:15; 25:7; Joshua 20:4; Ruth 4:1). Since Daniel was Prime Minister, it stands to reason he would remain at the royal court to take care of royal business. Daniel's fidelity to the God of heaven certainly tells us if he had been there he would have stood with his friends.

3:26–30 Faithfulness Rewarded

26. Then Nebuchadnezzar went near the mouth of the burning fiery furnace and spoke, saying, "Shadrach, Meshach, and Abed-Nego, servants of the Most High God, come out, and come here." Then Shadrach, Meshach, and Abed-Nego came from the midst of the fire. 27. And the satraps, administrators, governors, and the king's counselors gathered together, and they saw these men on whose bodies the fire had no power; the hair of their head was not singed nor were their garments affected, and the smell of fire was not on them. 28. Nebuchadnezzar spoke, saying, "Blessed be the God of Shadrach, Meshach, and Abed-Nego, who sent His Angel and delivered His servants who trusted in Him, and they have frustrated the king's word, and yielded their bodies, that they should not serve nor worship any god except their own

God! 29. "Therefore I make a decree that any people, nation, or language which speaks anything amiss against the God of Shadrach, Meshach, and Abed-Nego shall be cut in pieces, and their houses shall be made an ash heap; because there is no other God who can deliver like this." 30. Then the king promoted Shadrach, Meshach, and Abed-Nego in the province of Babylon.

Chapter 4

Nebuchadnezzar's Conversion

INSIDE THIS CHAPTER:

4:1–3 Nebuchadnezzar's Proclamation

1. Nebuchadnezzar the king, To all peoples, nations and languages that dwell in all the earth: Peace be multiplied to you. 2. I thought it good to declare the signs and wonders that the Most High God has worked for me. 3. How great are His signs, And how mighty His wonders! His kingdom is an everlasting kingdom, And His dominion is from generation to generation.

4:4–7 Nebuchadnezzar's Vision

4. I, Nebuchadnezzar, was at rest in my house, and flourishing in my palace. 5. I saw a dream which made me afraid, and the thoughts on my bed and the visions of my head troubled me. 6. Therefore I issued a decree to bring in all the wise men of Babylon before me, that they might make known to me the interpretation of the dream. 7. Then the magicians, the astrologers, the Chaldeans, and the soothsayers came in, and I told them the dream; but they did not make known to me its interpretation.

4:8, 9 Daniel Called

8. But at last Daniel came before me (his name is Belteshazzar, according to the name of my god; in him is the Spirit of the Holy God), and I told the dream before him, saying: 9. Belteshazzar, chief of the magicians, because I know that the Spirit of the Holy God is in you, and no secret troubles you, explain to me the visions of my dream that I have seen, and its interpretation.

4:8, 9 DANIEL CHIEF OF THE MAGICIANS

Consider This

Chapter 4 of Daniel is probably one of the greatest chapters in the Word of God. Here is recorded a testimony by one of earth's most outstanding kings, telling of his pride, humiliation and conversion. Daniel has been serving as the Prime Minister of Babylon (2:48). Through the providence of God, the wise men arrived before Daniel, made their attempt to interpret the dream, and failed. The main purpose of the dream was for Nebuchadnezzar to recognize the God of Heaven as the One who rules over men. Only after the Babylonian soothsayers had tried and failed, could Daniel show that his God was the only true God. Daniel came in at last, much to Nebuchadnezzar's relief. The Scripture makes it quite clear that the king had complete confidence in Daniel and his ability to interpret the dream.

4:10–19 The Great Tree

10. "These were the visions of my head while on my bed: I was looking, and behold, a tree in the midst of the earth, and its height was great. 11. The tree grew and became strong; its height reached to the heavens, and it could be seen to the ends of the earth. 12. Its leaves were lovely, its fruit abundant, and in it was food for all. The beasts of the field found shade under it, the birds of the heavens dwelt in its branches, and all flesh was fed from it. 13. "I saw in the visions of my head while on my bed, and there was a watcher, a holy one, coming down from heaven. 14. He cried aloud and said thus: 'Chop down the tree and cut off its branches, strip off its leaves and scatter its fruit. Let the beasts get out from under it, and the birds from its branches. 15. Nevertheless leave the stump and roots in the earth, bound with a band of iron and bronze, in the tender grass of the field. Let it be wet with the dew of heaven, and let him graze with the beasts on the grass of the earth. 16. Let his heart be changed from that of a man, let him be given the heart of a beast, and let seven times pass over him. 17. This decision is by the decree of the watchers, and the sentence by the word of the holy ones, in order that the living may know that the Most High rules in the kingdom of men, gives it to whomever He will, and sets over it the lowest of men.' 18. "This dream I, king Nebuchadnezzar, have seen. Now you, Belteshazzar, declare its interpretation, since all the wise men of my kingdom are not able to make known to me the interpretation; but you are able, for the Spirit of the Holy God is in you." 19. Then Daniel, whose name was Belteshazzar, was astonished for a time, and his thoughts troubled him. So the king spoke, and said, "Belteshazzar, do not let the dream or its interpretation trouble you." Belteshazzar

answered and said, "My lord, *may* the dream concern those who hate you, and its interpretation concern your enemies!"

4:10–19 NEBUCHADNEZZAR'S DREAM

Consider This

Nebuchadnezzar is recognized as one of the great builders of antiquity. In a very short time he brought Babylon to the place that it was looked upon as the golden kingdom. Proud and haughty, he believed that his kingdom reached to the ends of the earth. Thus God used a tree whose top reached to Heaven and could be seen from the ends of the earth to represent the kingdom of Babylon. Its leaves brought shelter and its fruit—food for all mankind. The cutting down of the tree, and not uprooting it, but leaving the stump with bands around it showed the kingdom of Babylon would continue. The bands of iron and brass were used by God to show that Babylon's influence would continue even into the kingdoms of Greece and Rome as represented in the image of Daniel 2. In fact, the stump and roots of the tree point to the enduring influence of Babylonian government and paganism upon man until the end of time. That is why the book of Revelation picks up the call to "… come out of Babylon my people" (Revelation 18:1–5). Since the kingdom of Babylon only lasted seventy years and Nebuchadnezzar ruled forty of them, this dream referred to him, but also to the kingdom as a whole.

4:20–26 Daniel Interprets the Dream

20. The tree that you saw, which grew and became strong, whose height reached to the heavens and which could be seen by all the earth, 21. whose leaves were lovely and its fruit abundant, in which was food for all, under which the beasts of the field dwelt, and on whose branches the birds of the heaven had their habitation— 22. it is you, O king, who have grown and become strong; for your greatness has grown and reaches to the heavens, and your dominion to the end of the earth. 23. And inasmuch as the king saw a watcher, a holy one, coming down from heaven and

saying, `Chop down the tree and destroy it, but leave its stump and roots in the earth, bound with a band of iron and bronze in the tender grass of the field; let it be wet with the dew of heaven, and let him graze with the beasts of the field, till seven times pass over him. 24. This is the interpretation, O king, and this is the decree of the Most High, which has come upon my lord the king: 25. They shall drive you from men, your dwelling shall be with the beast of the field, and they shall make you eat grass like oxen. They shall wet you with the dew of heaven, and seven times shall pass over you, till you know that the Most High rules in the kingdom of men, and gives it to whomever He chooses. 26. And inasmuch as they gave the command to leave the stump and roots of the tree, your kingdom shall be assured to you, after you come to know that Heaven rules.

4:20–23 TALE OF TWO CITIES

Consider This

In English literature there's a story told of two cities, one in England and one in France. The Bible pictures two cities throughout its pages, Jerusalem and Babylon. Jerusalem stands for peace found in Jesus Christ; whereas, Babylon represents confusion built on man's devising. Nebuchadnezzar felt that his kingdom had been built by his might and power. Anytime denominations, nations, man's ideology or educational institutions exalt human effort as self-sufficient, then you have the very spirit of Babylon.

4:24–26 EAT GRASS LIKE AN OX

Consider This

Psychiatrists call this lycanthropy, a disease that changes the behavior of man to that of a beast. To modern-day man there is an explanation for everything. But the fact remains that God decreed it and according to His Word it came to pass. It doesn't matter what man calls it. For seven years the king would live like an animal. Daniel uses the expression "… seven times" (4:25). This way of expressing time is also used later in Daniel where it mentions a "time, times and a half of time": a "time" represents one year (See p. 18 and "Closer Look" 7:24, 25).

4:27 God's Promise

27. Therefore, O king, let my counsel be acceptable to you; break off your sins by being righteous, and your iniquities by showing mercy to the poor. Perhaps there may be a lengthening of your prosperity.

4:27 GOD'S PROMISES AND CONDITIONS

Key to Prophecy

When God makes a promise concerning good and evil it is always given on condition. This point is extremely important to those who would understand Bible prophecy. "The instant I speak concerning a nation and concerning a kingdom, to pluck up, to pull down, and to destroy it. If that nation against whom I have spoken turns from its evil, I will relent of the disaster that I thought to bring upon it. And the instant I speak concerning a nation and concerning a kingdom, to build and to plant it. If it does evil in My sight so that it does not obey My voice, then I will relent concerning the good with which I said I would benefit it" (Jeremiah 18:7–10).

4:28–30 City of Babylon

28. All this came upon King Nebuchadnezzar. 29. At the end of the twelve months he was walking about the royal palace of Babylon. 30. The king spoke, saying, "Is not this great Babylon, that I have built for a royal dwelling by my mighty power and for the honor of my majesty?"

4:28–30 CITY OF BABYLON

Closer Look

Babylon is an old city dating back to the time of Nimrod, who first built it (Genesis 10:10). When Abraham left southern Mesopotamia about 2000 B.C., Babylon was a flourishing city (Genesis 11:27–31). You will find the ruins of the city in the country of Iraq, about fifty miles south of Baghdad on the Euphrates river. Babylon became the capital of the Neo-Babylonian Empire in 605 B.C., when Nabopolassar took over the Assyrian Empire. It was under King Nebuchadnezzar that Babylon reached the height of its splendor. He enlarged the city to an area of about 13 miles long and 10 miles wide. Around the city was a double wall some 50 feet thick, with 250 towers and eight gates. The most famous was the Ishtar Gate which opened to a sacred processional way leading to the temple of the pagan god Marduk. The gate and city walls were decorated with yellow, green and red-colored glazed bricks, which featured drawings of lions, dragons and bulls, on a background of blue. The center of Babylon's glory was the famous temple tower, Etemenanki, which was 300 feet square at the base and over 300 feet high.

One of the Seven Wonders of the ancient world was the famous hanging gardens that Nebuchadnezzar built for his wife. Since Babylon was set on the plains, and his wife was from the mountain country, the hanging gardens were to remind her of her mountain home.

In the northwest corner of the inner city was the Southern Palace. This was more or less the official residence of the king. This was where all the ceremonies of the state took place. In the center was a large throne room, 173 feet long, 57 feet wide and 66 feet high. This immense hall was probably where Belshazzar's feast took place and the handwriting on the wall appeared in Daniel 5:5. Nebuchadnezzar wanted the city of Babylon to last forever. Archaeologists have found bricks with this inscription on them, "The city which is the delight of my eyes, may it last forever". God had prophesied otherwise. (See Isaiah 13:19–21.)

4:31–33 Nebuchadnezzar's Humiliation

31. While the word was still in the king's mouth, a voice fell from heaven: "King Nebuchadnezzar, to you it is spoken: the kingdom

has departed from you! 32. And they shall drive you from men and your dwelling shall be with the beasts of the field. They shall make you eat grass like oxen; and seven times shall pass over you, until you know that the Most High rules in the kingdom of men, and gives it to whomever He chooses." 33. That very hour the word was fulfilled concerning Nebuchadnezzar; he was driven from men and ate grass like oxen; his body was wet with the dew of heaven till his hair had grown like eagle's feathers and his nails like birds' claws.

4:31–33 NEBUCHADNEZZAR'S HUMILIATION

Consider This

God's judgments against men can be halted by repentance and conversion (See Isaiah 38:1, 2, 5; Jonah 3:1–10). God announced the impending judgment upon Nebuchadnezzar for this reason. He gave him a full year to repent and avoid the threatened calamity (See 4:29). The king did not change his way of life, and thus brought upon himself the execution of this judgment.

4:34–37 Nebuchadnezzar's Conversion

34. And at the end of the time I, Nebuchadnezzar, lifted my eyes to heaven, and my understanding returned to me; and I blessed the Most High and praised and honored Him who lives forever: For His dominion is an everlasting dominion, and His kingdom is from generation to generation. 35. All the inhabitants of the earth are reputed as nothing; He does according to His will in the army of heaven, and among the inhabitants of the earth. No one can restrain His hand or say to Him, "What have You done?" 36. At the same time my reason returned to me, and for the glory of my kingdom, my honor and splendor returned to me. My counselors and nobles resorted to me, I was restored to my kingdom and excellent majesty was added to me. 37. Now I, Nebuchadnezzar, praise and extol and honor the King of heaven,

all of whose works are truth, and His ways justice. And those who walk in pride He is able to abase.

4:34–37 CHANGE OF HEART

Consider This

Marvelous grace, that a king as haughty and ruthless as Nebuchadnezzar could find mercy. What hope it offers to you and me. Daniel faithfully witnessed to Nebuchadnezzar and the king now accepted, recognized and worshiped the King of Heaven.

Chapter 5

The Fall of Babylon

INSIDE THIS CHAPTER:

5:1, 2 Belshazzar's Contempt of God

1. Belshazzar the king made a great feast for a thousand of his lords, and drank wine in the presence of the thousand. 2. While he tasted the wine, Belshazzar gave the command to bring the gold and silver vessels which his father Nebuchadnezzar had taken from the temple which had been in Jerusalem, that the king and his lords, his wives, and his concubines might drink from them.

5:2 GRANDSON LOSES KINGDOM

Closer Look

The term "father" was used when referring to a person's father or grandfather. Nebuchadnezzar's son-in-law was Nabonidus, and Belshazzar was Nabonidus' eldest son. From archeological information we learn that Nabonidus and Belshazzar were co-regents of Babylon. Nabonidus didn't like living in Babylon and wanted to be with the army, so he made his son co-ruler of Babylon. That's why in verse 7 Belshazzar says that the person who interpreted the handwriting on the wall would be made third in the kingdom. Nabonidus conducted a successful military expedition against the Arabian city, Tema, and made it his residence until Cyrus captured Babylon in 539 B.C. (See Map on p. 11).

5:3, 4 Sacred Vessels

3. Then they brought the gold vessels that had been taken from the temple of the house of God which had been in Jerusalem; and the king and his lords, his wives, and his concubines drank from them. 4. They drank wine, and praised the gods of gold and silver, bronze and iron, wood and stone.

5:3, 4 SACRED VESSELS

Consider This

The temple vessels had been dedicated to the Lord to be used in the service of the Sanctuary. They were always treated with utmost respect and reverence. Even Nebuchadnezzar treated them with esteem. When Belshazzar drank intoxicating drinks from them in worship to a false god, this was an insulting sacrilege and the God of Israel pulled down the curtain on the kingdom of Babylon.

5:5–9 Handwriting Shakes Up the King

5. In the same hour the fingers of a man's hand appeared and wrote opposite the lamp stand on the plaster of the wall of the king's palace; and the king saw the part of the hand that wrote. 6. Then the king's countenance changed, and his thoughts troubled him, so that the joints of his hips were loosened and his knees knocked against each other. 7. The king cried aloud to bring in the astrologers, the Chaldeans, and the soothsayers. And the king spoke, saying to the wise men of Babylon, "Whoever reads this writing and tells me its interpretation, shall be clothed with purple and have a chain of gold around his neck; and he shall be the third ruler in the kingdom." 8. Now all the king's wise men came, but they could not read the writing, or make known to the king its interpretation. 9. Then King Belshazzar was greatly troubled, his countenance was changed, and his lords were astonished.

5:10–25 Daniel Explains the Handwriting

10. The queen, because of the words of the king and his lords, came to the banquet hall. And the queen spoke, saying, "O king, live forever! Do not let your thoughts trouble you, nor let your countenance change. 11. "There is a man in your kingdom in whom is the Spirit of the Holy God. And in the days of your father, light and understanding and wisdom, like the wisdom of the gods, were found in him; and King Nebuchadnezzar your father—your father the king—made him chief of the magicians, astrologers, Chaldeans, and soothsayers. 12. Inasmuch as an excellent spirit, knowledge, understanding, interpreting dreams, solving riddles, and explaining enigmas were found in this Daniel whom the king named Belteshazzar, now let Daniel be called, and he will give the interpretation. 13. Then Daniel was brought

in before the king. And the king spoke, and said to Daniel, "Are you that Daniel who is one of the captives from Judah, whom my father the king brought from Judah? 14. "I have heard of you, that the Spirit of God is in you, and that light and understanding and excellent wisdom are found in you. 15. "Now the wise men, the astrologers, have been brought in before me, that they should read this writing and make known to me its interpretation, but they could not give the interpretation of the thing. 16. "And I have heard of you, that you can give interpretations and explain enigmas. Now if you can read the writing and make known to me its interpretation, you shall be clothed with purple and have a chain of gold around your neck, and shall be the third ruler in the kingdom."

5:10–16 OLD BUT NOT FORGOTTEN

Consider This

The queen mentioned here is no doubt the mother of Belshazzar. According to Oriental custom, none but a ruling monarch's mother would dare enter the presence of a king without being summoned. As a child she had seen and heard many of the events in which Daniel and her father, Nebuchadnezzar, were involved. According to archeological discoveries, Belshazzar's grandmother died in 547 B.C. After Nebuchadnezzar's memory and kingdom had been restored, he lived only a few more years. His son and grandson took over the leadership and a new regime came into power. The policy of righteousness and justice that Daniel stood for came into disfavor and he was retired from public service. The fact that Daniel later entered the service of Persia shows that his retirement at the close of the Babylonian Empire was not due to old age or ill health. Faced with the crisis of the handwriting on the wall, and the inability of the wise men to interpret it, the queen clearly remembered Daniel and how he had counseled and advised King Nebuchadnezzar. Daniel's straight reprimand of Belshazzar's lifestyle and policies showed his disapproval of how the affairs of state were being conducted.

5:17–25 Daniel Confronts Belshazzar

17. Then Daniel answered, and said before the king, "Let your gifts be for yourself, and give your rewards to another; yet I will read the writing to the king, and make known to him the interpretation. 18. "O King, the Most High God gave Nebuchadnezzar your father a kingdom and majesty, glory and honor. 19. "And because of the majesty that He gave him, all peoples, nations, and languages trembled and feared before him. Whomever he wished, he executed; whomever he wished, he kept alive; whomever he wished, he set up; and whomever he wished, he put down. 20. But when his heart was lifted up, and his spirit was hardened in pride, he was deposed from his kingly throne, and they took his glory from him. 21. Then he was driven from the sons of men, his heart was made like the beasts, and his dwelling was with the wild donkeys. They fed him with grass like oxen, and his body was wet with the dew of heaven, till he knew that the Most High God rules in the kingdom of men, and appoints over it whomever He chooses. 22. But you his son, Belshazzar, have not humbled your heart, although you knew all this. 23. "But you have lifted yourself up against the Lord of heaven. They have brought the vessels of His house before you, and you and your lords, your wives and your concubines, have drunk wine from them. And you have praised the gods of silver and gold, bronze and iron, wood and stone, which do not see or hear or know; and the God who holds your breath in His hand and owns all your ways, you have not glorified. 24. Then the fingers of the hand were sent from Him, and this writing was written. 25. And this is the inscription that was written: Mene, Mene, Tekel, Upharsin."

5:26–29 Mene, Mene, Tekel, Upharsin

26. "This is the interpretation of each word. **Mene:** God has numbered your kingdom and finished it: 27. "**Tekel:** You have been weighed in the balance, and found wanting. 28. "**Peres:** Your kingdom has been divided, and given to the Medes and Persians." 29. Then Belshazzar gave the command and they clothed Daniel

with purple and put a chain of gold around his neck, and made a proclamation concerning him that he should be the third ruler in the kingdom.

5:26–29 MENE, MENE, TEKEL, UPHARSIN

Closer Look

Mene is a form of the verb "to number", and means "numbered". *Teqel* is related to a verb meaning "to weigh" and the consonantal Aramaic term may be translated "weighed." The "*u*" in Upharsin is an Aramaic conjunction meaning "and," and when detached from upharsin the *pharsen* becomes *parsen* (RSV "parsin"). *Parsen* is the plural of *peres* and means "pieces." This explains the difference between *upharsin* and *peres*. The message may thus be interpreted as "numbered, numbered, weighed, pieces." This cryptic message, even if it could be deciphered, required an interpreter, and Daniel was eventually summoned to interpret the divine message.

5:30 Belshazzar Is Slain

30. That very night Belshazzar, king of the Chaldeans, was slain.

5:31 Medes and Persians Take Babylon

31. And Darius the Mede received the kingdom, being about sixty-two years old.

5:31 PROPHECY FULFILLED

Key to Prophecy

Darius was sixty-two years old when he took over the Babylonian Empire. He only lived two more years and then Cyrus became king. Daniel continued his service in the courts of Medo-Persia until the first year of Cyrus' reign. Babylon fell to Medo-Persia exactly as Daniel had prophesied 50 years before Cyrus was born. The Scripture foretold how he would overthrow the city of Babylon. No doubt Daniel showed this Scripture to Cyrus. This made an impact on Cyrus (Ezra 1:14), as he made the decree for the children of Israel to return to Jerusalem. Cyrus lived a charmed life. The magi told Cyrus' grandfather, Astyages the king, that the child would take over his kingdom. Because of this, his grandfather made several attempts on Cyrus' life.

The fact that the Persian account of the fall of Babylon to Cyrus begins his reign in Babylon immediately, without any intervening reign of Darius the Mede, does not contradict the Biblical narrative. Darius was evidently recognized as a ruler in Babylon by courtesy

of Cyrus, while it was Cyrus who actually held the power. The lack of conclusive evidence as to the identity of Darius the Mede must not be a cause to question the Bible statements concerning this ruler, for future finds may clarify the problem, as archeology has already done for Belshazzar, who puzzled earlier historians.

Chapter 6

Daniel in the Lions' Den

INSIDE THIS CHAPTER:

6:1, 2 Daniel Prime Minister Again

1. It pleased Darius to set over the kingdom one hundred and twenty satraps, to be over the whole kingdom: 2. and over these, three governors, of whom Daniel was one, that the satraps might give account to them, so that the king would suffer no loss.

6:3 Daniel's Excellent Spirit

3. Then this Daniel distinguished himself above the governors and satraps, because an excellent spirit was in him; and the king gave thought to setting him over the whole realm.

6:3 TOTALLY UNIQUE

Consider This

This is not the first time this excellent spirit is seen in Daniel. Nebuchadnezzar observed it, (4:8), and the queen mother referred to the same quality (5:11, 12). He was unwavering in faithfulness, loyal to duty, and showed unquestionable integrity in words and acts. Those were qualities not seen in public servants of that age.

6:4–9 A Foolish Decree

4. So the governors and satraps sought to find some charge against Daniel concerning the kingdom; but they could find no charge or fault, because he was faithful; nor was there any error or fault found in him. 5. Then these men said, "We shall not find any charge against this Daniel unless we find it against him concerning the law of his God." 6. So these governors and satraps thronged before the king, and said thus to him; "King Darius, live forever! 7. "All the governors of the kingdom, the administrators and satraps, the counselors and advisors, have consulted together to establish a royal statute and to make a firm decree, that whoever petitions any god or man for thirty days, except you, O king, shall be cast into the den of lions. 8. "Now, O king, establish the decree and sign the writing, so that it cannot be changed, according to the law of the Medes and Persians, which does not alter." 9. Therefore King Darius signed the written decree.

6:10, 11 Daniel's Lifestyle Unchanged

10. Now when Daniel knew that the writing was signed, he went home. And in his upper room, with his windows open toward Jerusalem, he knelt down on his knees three times that day, and prayed and gave thanks before his God, as was his custom since early days. 11. Then these men assembled and found Daniel praying and making supplication before his God.

#4 Faith Builder

Faith Builders   **Next Faith Builder**   **#5 Chapter 9:3, 4**

6:10,11 POWER OF A FAITHFUL WITNESS

There are situations in the life of Daniel which give us indications of how he built his faith. Hebrews 11:6 says, "Without faith you cannot please God". The six examples in this book of how he built his faith are needed in today's hectic society.

God does not ask us to handle the circumstances of our lives. He only asks that we commit our lives to Him and He will handle the circumstances. Faith means simply resting in God's care.

Under the new regime, Daniel's lifestyle of praying three times a day did not change. Faith makes a person's witnessing consistent with his belief. Daniel was living proof that he trusted his God to take care of any circumstances, regardless of the outcome.

6:12–15 The Governors and Satraps Accuse Daniel

12. And they went before the king, and spoke concerning the king's decree: "Have you not signed a decree that every man who petitions any god or man within thirty days, except you, O king, shall be cast into the den of lions?" The king answered and said, "The thing is true, according to the law of the Medes and Persians,

which does not alter." 13. So they answered and said before the king, "That Daniel, who is one of the captives from Judah, does not show due regard for you, O king, or for the decree that you have signed, but makes his petition three times a day." 14. And the king, when he heard these words, was greatly displeased with himself, and set his heart on Daniel to deliver him; and he labored till the going down of the sun to deliver him. 15. Then these men approached the king and said to the king, "Know, O king, that it is the law of the Medes and Persians that no decree or statute which the king establishes may be changed."

6:16–19 Daniel in the Lions' Den

16. So the king gave the command, and they brought Daniel and cast him into the den of lions. But the king spoke, saying to Daniel, "Your God, whom you serve continually, He will deliver you." 17. Then a stone was brought and laid on the mouth of the den, and the king sealed it with his own signet ring and with the signets of his lords, that the purpose concerning Daniel might not be changed. 18. Now the king went to his palace and spent the night fasting; and no musicians were brought before him. Also his sleep went from him. 19. Then the king arose very early in the morning and went in haste to the den of lions.

6:20 The King Calls to Daniel

20. And when he came to the den, he cried out with a lamenting voice to Daniel. The king spoke, saying to Daniel, "Daniel, servant of the living God, has your God, whom you serve continually, been able to deliver you from the lions?"

6:20 THE KING CALLS TO DANIEL

Consider This

Darius' words, "… the living God" (6:20), show he had become acquainted with Daniel's belief in a God not made of gold, wood or stone. The same witness Daniel had so faithfully shown to Nebuchadnezzar was now impressing Darius, that there was a God in heaven who rules in the affairs of men.

6:21–24 God Shuts the Lions' Mouths

21. Then Daniel said to the king, "O king live forever! 22. "My God sent His angel and shut the lions' mouths, so that they have not hurt me, because I was found innocent before Him; and also, O king, I have done no wrong before you." 23. Then the king was exceedingly glad for him, and commanded that they should take Daniel up out of the den. So Daniel was taken up out of the den, and no injury whatever was found on him, because he believed in his God. 24. And the king gave the command, and they brought those men who had accused Daniel, and they cast them into the den of lions—them, their children, and their wives, and the lions overpowered them, and broke all their bones in pieces before they ever came to the bottom of the den.

6:25–28 Darius Magnifies God

25. Then King Darius wrote: To all peoples, nations, and languages that dwell in all the earth: Peace be multiplied to you. 26. I make a decree that in every dominion of my

kingdom men must tremble and fear before the God of Daniel. For He is the living God, And steadfast forever; His kingdom is the one which shall not be destroyed, And His dominion shall endure to the end. 27. He delivers and rescues, and He works signs and wonders in heaven and on earth, Who has delivered Daniel from the power of the lions. 28. So this Daniel prospered in the reign of Darius and in the reign of Cyrus the Persian.

Key to Prophecy

The Bible Prophecy Principle of "Repeat and Enlarge"

The next six chapters of Daniel reveal what God showed him in visions and dreams. These revelations were given at different times during his life. <u>One of the important principles to know in understanding Bible prophecy is the rule of "repeat and enlarge." During the reading of the next six prophecies you will see how the Lord repeats and enlarges our understanding of the events covering the period of time from Daniel's day to the Second Coming of Christ.</u> In Daniel 7, God repeats what was given in Daniel 2, which are the foundation blocks of the later prophecies. He then enlarges the last part, which makes the picture more complete. The understanding of these prophecies has been progressive as the events have taken place. Jesus said, "These things have been spoken unto you that, when they come to pass, ye may believe" (John 14:29). You will want to look at the chart located After chapter 7 as you examine these prophecies.

Chapter 7

Four Great Beasts

INSIDE THIS CHAPTER:

7:1–8 Four Great Beasts

1. In the first year of Belshazzar king of Babylon, Daniel had a dream and visions of his head while on his bed. Then he wrote down the dream, telling the main facts. 2. Daniel spoke, saying, "I saw in my vision by night, and behold, the four winds of heaven were stirring up the Great Sea.

7:2 PROPHETIC SYMBOLISM

Key to Prophecy

God uses water in Bible prophecy to represent people, nations and tongues. "And he said to me, 'The waters which you saw, where the harlot sits, are peoples, multitudes, nations, and tongues'" (Revelation 17:15). In Jeremiah 49:35–37, wind is used to symbolize war and strife. "After these things I saw four angels standing at the four corners of the earth, holding the four winds of the earth, that the wind should not blow on the earth, or the sea, or on any tree" (Revelation 7:1).

3. "And four great beasts came up from the sea, each different from the other.

7:3 BEASTS IN BIBLE PROPHECY

Key to Prophecy

Beasts in Bible prophecy represent nations, just as an eagle is used to symbolize the United States, and a lion to depict England. "Those great beasts, which are four, are four kings which arise out of the earth" (7:17),

4. "The first was like a lion, and had eagle's wings. I watched till its wings were plucked off; and it was lifted up from the earth and made to stand on two feet like a man, and a man's heart was given to it."

7:4 BABYLON AS A LION

Closer Look

Babylon is pictured as a lion in Jeremiah 4:7. The lion was used historically to represent Babylon. When the British Museum excavated the ruins of Babylon, they found statues of lions with eagle's wings. The wings represent the speed with which it conquered (See "Terms for Your Tour Explained" on p. 18). "Plucked off" shows that its conquering ceased. Babylon overthrew Assyria in 605 B.C.

Nebuchadnezzar ruled forty of the seventy years the kingdom existed. Because of Nebuchadnezzar's conversion the lion is pictured as having a man's heart. The lion corresponds to the head of gold in Daniel 2.

5. "And suddenly another beast, a second, like a bear. It was raised up on one side, and had three ribs in its mouth between its teeth. And they said thus to it: 'Arise, devour much flesh.'"

7:5 MEDO-PERSIA AS A BEAR

Closer Look

Babylon fell to Medo-Persia in 539 B.C. Medo-Persia corresponds to the silver of the image of Daniel 2. Darius the Mede and Cyrus the Persian had formed an alliance to overthrow Babylon. The Bear, raised on one side, represents Persia, the stronger of the two countries. The three ribs in its mouth represent the nations overthrown by the Bear (Medo-Persia). They were Egypt 535 B.C., Babylon 539 B.C. and Lydia 546 B.C. The Ram of chapter 8 is this same power and God will repeat and enlarge so there is no doubt as to its identity.

6. "After this I looked, and there was another, like a leopard, which had on its back four wings of a bird. The beast also had four heads, and dominion was given to it."

7:6 GREECE AS A LEOPARD

Closer Look

Alexander the Great met Darius on the plains of Arbela in 331 B.C. The leopard and the bronze of the image of Daniel 2 depict the kingdom of Greece. The four wings represent the swiftness with which Alexander conquered the world (See "Closer Look" 2:39B). By age thirty, Alexander had nothing else to conquer. Returning from his campaign, suffering from malaria and drunkenness, and knowing he was dying, he called for his four generals. They asked to whom he would give the empire. He responded by saying, "to the strongest". At his death his kingdom was divided among his four generals. This is why the leopard has four heads. The Goat of chapter 8 expands on the explanation of this beast and leaves no doubt as to its identity.

7. "After this I saw in the night visions, and behold, a fourth beast, dreadful and terrible, exceedingly strong. It had huge iron teeth; it was devouring, breaking in pieces, and trampling the residue with its feet. It was different from all the beasts that were before it, and it had ten horns.

7:7 PAGAN ROME THE TERRIBLE BEAST

Closer Look

The fourth beast with iron teeth is the same as the legs of iron in Daniel 2. The takeover of the Grecian Empire was slow, but by 168 B.C., the Romans were very much in control. The great iron teeth portray the way Rome devoured nations and people in its conquests. What Rome did not destroy she brought into slavery, as the Scripture describes, "… trampling the residue with its feet" (7:7). Rome ruled until A.D. 476, at which time the Germanic tribes invaded the Roman Empire, breaking it into pieces, and finally into ten parts. The ten horns represent the tribes corresponding to the toes of the image in Daniel 2 (See "Closer Look" 2:41–43). Remember, God will repeat and enlarge in later chapters.

8. "I was considering the horns, and there was another horn, a little one, coming up among them, before whom three of the first horns were plucked out by the roots. And there, in this horn, were eyes like the eyes of a man, and a mouth speaking pompous words.

7:8 THE LITTLE HORN

Closer Look

The Scripture lists four points that identify the Little Horn:

1. "Coming up among them" — the Little Horn would arise among the ten horns of Western Europe.

2. "Before whom three of the first horns were plucked out by the roots"—three of these Germanic tribes would be destroyed. (See "Closer Look" 2:41–43.)

3. "Eyes like the eyes of a man"—referring to its leadership.

4. "A mouth speaking pompous words"—V. 25 says, "against the Most High." This power will speak words against God. The Little Horn is identified in greater detail in verses 24, 25 where these and other points will be explained.

7:9, 10 Judgment Scene

9. "I watched till thrones were put in place, and the Ancient of Days was seated; His garment was white as snow, and the hair of His head was like pure wool. His throne was a fiery flame, its wheels a burning fire; 10. "A fiery stream issued and came forth from before Him. A thousand thousands ministered to Him; ten thousand times ten thousand stood before Him. The court was seated, and the books were opened."

7:9, 10 COURT IN SESSION

Closer Look

This time of judgment will take place at the close of the Little Horn's power, according to verse 26. Daniel is being shown different scenes. This is why he repeats, "… I watched" (7:9). He has been taken from the actions of the Little Horn to the Courtroom in Heaven. There are three books used in the judgment: 1) The Book of Life, (Revelation 20:12), listing the names of all who have accepted Christ; 2) The Book of Remembrance (Malachi 3:16), recording the good deeds of all; 3) The Book of Iniquity (Isaiah 65:6, 7), recording the sins of men. For a more complete study of the judgment, refer to 9:23–27.

7:11, 12 Rise and Fall of Nations

11. "I watched then because of the sound of the pompous words which the horn was speaking; I watched till the beast was slain, and its body destroyed and given to the burning flame. 12. "As for the rest of the beasts, they had their dominion taken away, yet their lives were prolonged for a season and a time."

7:11, 12 RISE AND FALL OF NATIONS

Closer Look

Daniel is shown the end of the system symbolized by the Little Horn, which is destroyed at the Second Coming of Christ. The other beasts which represented nations were overthrown but allowed to live on. For instance when Persia overthrew Babylon the subjects of Babylon were allowed to live on. For this reason verse 12 says, "... yet their lives were prolonged for a season and a time" (7:12).

7:13, 14 Christ the Mediator

13. "I was watching in the night visions, and behold, One like the Son of Man, coming with the clouds of heaven! He came to the Ancient of Days, and they brought him near before Him. 14. Then to Him was given dominion and glory and a kingdom, that all peoples, nations, and languages should serve Him. His dominion is an everlasting dominion, which shall not pass away, and His kingdom the one which shall not be destroyed."

7:13, 14 CHRIST THE MEDIATOR

Consider This

This passage cannot be referring to the Second Coming of Christ to this earth; instead, He is coming to the "... Ancient of Days" (7:13). Daniel was shown that at the end of the rule of the Little Horn, judgment would begin in heaven (7:26, 27). Jesus said, "And behold, I am coming quickly, and My reward is with Me, to give to every one according to his work" (Revelation 22:12). Since He brings His reward with Him, each case has to have been decided. The Scripture says Christ intercedes for us. He is our Mediator (1 Timothy 2:5), High Priest (Hebrews 2:17), and Advocate (1 John 2:1). Daniel is shown a scene of Christ coming before His Father to intercede on our behalf during the judgment. At the close of the judgment the kingdom and all dominion will be given to Christ (7:14). Then He will come a second time to claim His people.

7:15, 16 Explanation Given to Daniel

15. "I, Daniel, was grieved in my spirit within my body, and the visions of my head troubled me. 16. "I came near to one of those who stood by, and asked him the truth of all this. So he told me and made known to me the interpretation of these things;

7:17 The Interpretation

17. "Those great beasts, which are four, are four kings which arise out of the earth.

7:17 BEAST IDENTIFIED

Key to Prophecy

In Bible prophecy, beasts represent nations or kings. The four beasts pictured in Daniel 7 are Babylon, Medo-Persia, Greece and Pagan Rome as we have just learned.

7:18–21 What About the Fourth Beast?

18. But the saints of the Most High shall receive the kingdom, and possess the kingdom forever, even forever and ever. 19. "Then I wished to know the truth about the fourth beast, which was different from all the others, exceedingly dreadful, with its teeth of iron and its nails of bronze, which devoured, broke in pieces, and trampled the residue with its feet; 20. "And about the ten horns that were on its head, and about the other horn which came up, before which three fell, namely, that horn which had eyes and a mouth which spoke pompous words, whose appearance was greater than his fellows. 21. "I was watching, and the same horn was making war against the saints, and prevailing against them."

7:22 The Saints Win

22. "Until the Ancient of Days came, and a judgment was made in favor of the saints of the Most High, and the time came for the saints to possess the kingdom."

7:22 THE SAINTS WIN

Closer Look

The Little Horn persecuted the followers of Christ until the judgment began. In verse 21, it looks as if the Little Horn will win. Then the "Son of Man" (7:13) appears in the presence of the Ancient of Days and judgment is turned over to Him. "For the Father judges no one, but has committed all judgment to the

Son, that all should honor the Son just as they honor the Father, he who does not honor the Son does not honor the Father who sent Him" (John 5:22, 23). Christ met the demands of the law. He paid the penalty of death and lived a perfect life in accordance with the law. Because of His intercession, judgment is made in favor of the saints.

7:23–25 Little Horn Further Identified

23. "Thus he said: the fourth beast shall be a fourth kingdom on earth, which shall be different from all other kingdoms, and shall devour the whole earth, trample it and break it in pieces. The ten horns are ten kings who shall arise from this kingdom. And another shall rise after them; he shall be different from the first ones, and shall subdue three kings. 25. He shall speak pompous words against the Most High, shall persecute the saints of the Most High and shall intend to change times and law. Then the saints shall be given into his hand for a time and times and half a time."

7:23–25A LITTLE HORN IDENTIFIED

Closer Look

Here God, in His wisdom, gave nine points for identifying the Little Horn of Daniel 7. There is only one power in the history of mankind that fits these nine points. Listed below are the nine points with an explanation of each:

1. "Coming up among them" (7:8). The ten horns were the ten Germanic tribes who took over Pagan Rome. These Goths became the nations of Western Europe today. As an example, the Alamanni became Germany, the Franks became France, etc. (See "Closer Look" 2:41–43.) Therefore, this Little Horn would have to rise out of Western Europe, since it must come up among the ten horns.

2. "Another shall rise after them" (7:24). The ten Germanic tribes overthrew Rome in A.D. 476. The Little Horn would have to come on the scene of action after this time.

3. "He shall be different from the first ones" (7:24). The Barbarian tribes were pagans. This Little Horn was to be different from the ten. It had to be more than just a political power.

4. "Shall subdue three kings" (7:24). The Emperor of Rome, at this time, was Justinian. He saw his empire being taken away by the Goths who had overrun the kingdom. Three tribes, the Heruli, Vandals and Ostrogoths, had accepted a belief called Arianism, which taught that Jesus Christ was a good man but not divine. The Catholic Church was in opposition to this belief and Justinian joined forces with them to do away with these three tribes. In 7:8, it says, "… three would be plucked up by the roots." Today there are descendants of all the Germanic tribes except for the Heruli, Vandals and Ostrogoths, who were completely destroyed through the efforts of the Catholic Church and Pagan Rome. The last to be annihilated was the Ostrogoths in A.D. 538. With this victory, history says the Pope seized the scepter and stepped to the seat of Caesar. Thus began the reign of Papal Rome.

5. "Eyes like the eyes of a man" (7:8). Sometimes horns have crowns on them, meaning that powers or nations would be controlled by a king. These nine points will identify clearly the Little Horn as the Papal power. The Pope is the visible head of the Papacy, or the "eyes like the eyes of a man" (7:8), referring to the leadership of this man. (See "Terms For Your Tour" p. 18.)

6. "Speak pompous words against the Most High" (7:25). Most High, in this verse, refers to God, and each time it is used in Scripture it refers to God. The following are excerpts from a Catholic Encyclopedia entitled *Prompta Bibliotheca* Vol. VI, pp. 25–29:

> "The Pope is of so great dignity and so exalted that he is not a mere man, but as it were God, and the vicar of God."

> "The Pope is as it were, God on earth, sole sovereign of the faithful of Christ, chief of kings, having plentitude of power, to whom has been entrusted by the omnipotent God direction not only of the earthly but also of the heavenly kingdom."

"The Pope is of so great authority and power that he can modify, explain, or interpret even divine laws."

7. "Persecute the saints of the Most High" (7:25). Historians say the Papal Power has slain somewhere between 100 to 150 million people. Here is a list of history books which will tell you about the persecution of the Waldensian people, persecution of the Dutch, the Spanish Inquisition and the Massacre of Saint Bartholomew:

   - *The History of the Reformation* by D'Aubigne

   - *History of Europe* by Qualbin

   - *Foxe's Book of Martyrs* by Foxe

   - *Short Stories of the Reformation* by Short

   - *Here I Stand* by Bainton

   This is common knowledge, as on May 24, 1995, Pope John Paul II issued a world apology for the persecuting role of the Church during this time.

8. "Intend to change times and laws" (7:25). God is the One who predetermines the events of life. It is He who "… removes kings and raises up kings …" (2:21). The Little Horn power attempted to change the course of history, "times" (7:25), by exercising the prerogative of God in setting up kings and taking them down.

   Concerning changing "laws" (7:25), the Papal Power says, "The Pope can modify divine law, since his power is not of man, but of God" (*Prompta Bibliotheca*, Vol. VI, pp. 25–29). Comparing the ten commandments in a Catholic Catechism with Scripture will show that he has exercised that prerogative.

   The second commandment that says, "You shall not make unto thee any graven image …" (Exodus 20:4), has been removed causing the rest to be moved up. For example, they moved the fourth commandment to the third. In order to still have ten commandments they took the tenth commandment and divided it.

The fourth commandment that says, "Remember the Sabbath day to keep it holy …" (Exodus 20:8), has been completely changed. They shortened it from 94 words to 8 words. The seventh day that God blessed, hallowed and sanctified (See Genesis 2:3; Exodus 20:11), was done away with by the Catholic Church. In its place they put Sunday. They took the first day of the week, Sunday, a day dedicated to the worship of the sun, and replaced the Bible Sabbath.

"Perhaps the boldest thing, the most revolutionary change, the Church ever did happened in the first century. The holy day, the Sabbath, was changed from Saturday to Sunday … not from any directions noted in the Scriptures, but from the Church's sense of its own power … People who think that the Scriptures should be the sole authority, should logically become 7th Day Adventists, and keep Saturday holy" (*Saint Catherine Catholic Church Sentinel*, May 21, 1995).

1260 yrs

9. "Time and times and half a time" (7:25). God has given a rule in Bible prophecy that a day represents one year (Ezekiel 4:6; Numbers 14:34). In the Scripture, time represents one year (4:16). Using the principle of a day for a year, times would mean two years, and half a time would stand for half a year. There are 360 days in a biblical year.

The story of the Great Flood holds a key to this time-reckoning principle. Genesis 7:11 says that the flood began in the "… second month on the seventeenth day of the month" and Genesis 8:4 says that the waters abated and the ark rested on Mt. Ararat on the "… seventh month and the seventeenth day of the month." The second month to the seventh month makes five months. Genesis 7:24; 8:3 speak of that period of time as "… one hundred and fifty days."

If five months equal 150 days, one month would be 30 days (30 x 5 = 150). One year would be 360 days, two years would be 720 days, and half of a year would be 180 days, for a total of 1,260 days. Each day represents a year, giving us 1,260 years, in which the Little Horn was to be in power.

It came into power in A.D. 538. Adding 1,260 years to the date of A.D. 538, takes us to A.D. 1798. This time is known in history as the period of Papal Supremacy. In A.D. 1798 Napoleon's general marched into Rome and brought the Papal power to an end.

7:23–25B LITTLE HORN VERSUS GOD'S LAW

Closer Look

"Then the saints shall be given into his hand for a time and times and half a time" (7:25). The saints given into his hand means that the papal power would rule over them for a period of 1,260 years which was fulfilled in history during the time of Papal Supremacy from A.D. 538 to A.D. 1798 (See above). During this time the Church used civil power to carry out its demands and the believers suffered great persecution.

In Revelation 13, we find that the beast has the same identifying marks as the Little Horn of Daniel 7 (See 7:23–25; Revelation 13:5–15). This means that the Catholic Church will gain power again in the last days and will use the state to enforce its laws. The Scripture says that the beast will "… speak, and cause" (Revelation 13:15) the people to worship him. The words "speak" and "cause" mean to legislate and enforce.

The Ten Commandments are God's Law and great principles that give guidance to the way we live. The first four define our relationship to God and the last six our duty to our fellow man.

The first three commandments do not require an outward demonstration of our commitment to God. In our relationship with God it is the fourth commandment that requires us to set aside the seventh day as holy and to refrain from work. In other words, it affects our lifestyle. It would be very hard to legislate how one thinks and believes (i.e. the first three commandments). Since the keeping of Sunday rests on Papal authority and not on Scripture (i.e. God's authority), and is something that can be enforced, it will be upon this point that the beast power will demand allegiance. It is the fourth commandment of God's Law that the Catholic Church has changed and by continuing to champion this cause she will use civil power to enforce Sunday observance in the last days.

7:26, 27 Judgment to Begin

26. "But the court shall be seated, and they shall take away his dominion, to consume and destroy it forever. 27. Then the kingdom and dominion, and the greatness of the kingdoms under the whole heaven, shall be given to the people, the saints of the Most High. His kingdom is an everlasting kingdom, and all dominions shall serve and obey Him.

7:26, 27 JUDGMENT TO BEGIN

Closer Look

When the Papal Power reached its end in A.D. 1798 and its dominion was taken away, the judgment was to open in Heaven (Refer back to: "Closer Look" 7:9, 10; "Consider This" 7:13, 14).

7:28 Daniel Still Troubled

28. "This is the end of the account. As for me, Daniel, my thoughts greatly troubled me, and my countenance changed; but I kept the matter in my heart."

SUMMARY OF CHAPTER 7

Daniel 8, 9 are a continuation of Daniel 7. Each chapter adds more information and comes closer to the final scenes of earth's history. These chapters follow the Bible principal of repeat and enlarge.

PROPHECIES RE\[

	1.		2.		3.		4
605 B.C.		539 B.C.		331 B.C.		168 B.C.	

DAN. 2

Head of Gold	Arms & Chest of Silver	Belly of Brass	Legs o\[
Babylon Dan. 2:38	Medo-Persia Dan. 2:39	Greece Dan. 2:39	Pagan Dan. 2\[

DAN. 7

Lion	Bear	Leopard	Terrib\[
Babylon Dan. 7:4	Medo-Persia Dan. 7:5	Greece Dan. 7:6	Pagan Dan. 7\[

DAN. 8

	Ram Medo-Persia	Goat Greece	I____
	Dan. 8:20	Dan. 8:21	

DAN. 9

	457 B.C. Decree to Restore and build Jerusalem		27 A.I Baptis of Jesi Cru
	⌐70 Weeks or 490 Years Dan. 9:24		
	⌐69 Weeks or 483 Years Dan. 9:25 I_		
	I_____2300 Years of Daniel 8:14 then t		

DAN. 11

	Medo-Persia	Greece-Egypt King of the South and North	Pagan King ⦁ North
	Dan. 11:1,2	Dan. 11:3-13	Dan. 1\[

EALED TO DANIEL

538 A.D.	**5.**	1798 A.D.	**6.**	1991 A.D.	**7.**	END

Feet and Toes
Iron and Clay
Ten Divisions   "Days of these Kings"
Dan. 2:41-44   Dan. 2:44,45

1844 A.D.

st   Little Horn | Court is seated |
        1260 Years   Dan. 7:9,10
                                      Saints possess
        Papal Rome   the Kingdom
        Dan. 7:24,25   Dan. 7:22

| Little Horn   I
Both Pagan & Papal Rome
Dan. 8:9-12

A.D.   34 A.D.   1844 A.D.
 +   Gospel   Judgment begins
         to the Gentiles   in the Heavenly
n of Christ   Sanctuary

.9:27 |
Week |
nctuary will be Cleansed |

      Papal Rome   Atheism   Papal Rome
                        Spiritually Egypt   King of the
                        King of the South   North
                     | "Time of the End" |
0   Dan. 11:31-35   Dan. 11:36-39   Dan. 11:40-45

Chapter 8

The Ram and the Goat

INSIDE THIS CHAPTER:

INTRODUCTION TO CHAPTER 8

Closer Look

Two years after the prophecy of Daniel 7 foretold that the great empire of Babylon would fall, Daniel saw it happen. By the time of Daniel 8, Babylon as a world power was becoming history rather than prophecy. Thus, Daniel 8 begins with the second world power.

8:1–4 Vision of the Ram

1. In the third year of the reign of King Belshazzar a vision appeared to me—to me, Daniel—after the one that appeared to me the first time. 2. I saw in the vision, and it so happened while I was looking, that I was in Shushan, the citadel, which is in the province of Elam; and I saw in the vision that I was by the River Ulai. 3. Then I lifted my eyes and saw, and there, standing beside the river, was a ram which had two horns, and the two horns were high; but one was higher than the other, and the higher one came up last. 4. I saw the ram pushing westward, northward, and southward, so that no beast, could withstand him; nor was there any that could deliver from his hand, but he did according to his will and became great.

8:3, 4 MEDO-PERSIA THE RAM

Closer Look

Daniel 8:20 leaves no doubt as to who the Ram represents. "The ram which you saw, having the two horns—they are the kings of Media and Persia" (8:20). The two horns portray the joining of these two powers. The larger horn represents Persia, which came into the federation last but became the strongest of the two. The Medo-Persian Empire extended its border all the way from India to Ethiopia as prophesied. It pushed westward, northward and southward. The Persian monarch referred to himself as the "King of Kings." The countries of Egypt, Lydia and Babylon fell to the conquest of Medo-Persia. (See the bear in chapter 7 and the silver of the image in chapter 2.)

8:5-8 The Male Goat

5. And as I was considering, suddenly a male goat came from the west, across the surface of the whole earth, without touching the ground; and the goat had a notable horn between his eyes.

6. Then he came to the ram that had two horns, which I had seen standing beside the river, and ran at him with furious power. 7. And I saw him confronting the ram; he was moved with rage against him, attacked the ram, and broke his two horns. There was no power in the ram to withstand him, but he cast him down to the ground and trampled him; and there was no one that could deliver the ram from his hand. 8. Therefore the male goat grew very great, but when he became strong, the large horn was broken, and in place of it four notable ones came up toward the four winds of heaven.

8:5-8 GREECE THE MALE GOAT

Closer Look

Verses 21, 22 of this chapter identify the male goat. "And the male goat is the kingdom of Greece. The large horn between its eyes is the first king. As for the broken horn and the four that stood up in its place, four kingdoms shall arise out of that nation, but not with its power" (8:21, 22). Alexander the Great forged the Grecian Empire. The "... notable horn" (8:5), describes his leadership, and the goat "… without touching the ground" (8:5), describes the swiftness with which he conquered. "… The large horn was broken; and in place of it four notable ones came up" (8:8). Alexander died at the height of his power in 323 B.C. History reveals that Alexander's kingdom was divided among his four generals who lacked his strength. The description "… towards the four winds of heaven" (8:8), (see "Terms for Your Tour Explained" p. 16), was played out in history by each of Alexander's four leading generals receiving a portion of the Grecian Empire. Seleucus became ruler in the East over Syria, Lysimachus ruled in the North over Palestine, Cassander ruled in the West over Macedonia, and Ptolemy ruled in the South over Egypt.

8:9–12 The Little Horn

9. And out of one of them came a little horn which grew exceedingly great toward the south, toward the east, and toward the Glorious Land. 10. And it grew up to the host of heaven and it cast down some of the host and some of the stars to the ground, and trampled them. 11. He even exalted himself as high as the Prince of the host; and by him the daily sacrifices were taken away, and the place of His sanctuary was cast down. 12. Because of transgression, an army was given over to the horn to oppose the daily sacrifices; and he cast truth down to the ground. He did all this and prospered.

8:9-12 PAGAN AND PAPAL ROME

Closer Look

The phrase "… out of one of them came a Little Horn" (8:9), refers to the four winds in verse 8. Since the Little Horn power pushed to the south, east, and north, it had to come from the west. History records that Cassander's kingdom, pushed "… toward the south" (8:9), (Egypt fell to Rome in 30 B.C.), pushed "… toward the east" (8:9), (Syria fell to Rome in 65 B.C.), and pushed north "… toward the Glorious Land" (8:9) (Palestine fell to Rome in 63 B.C.). Of the four leading generals, Cassander proved to be the strongest. His kingdom grew to become the mighty Roman Empire, the "Little Horn, which grew exceeding great" (8:9).

MAP OF THE ROMAN EMPIRE

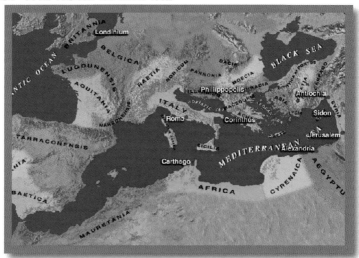

ANTIOCHUS EPIPHANES

Closer Look

In Daniel 2; 7; 8; 11, all the world empires appear in the same order: Babylon, Medo-Persia, Greece, Pagan Rome, the divided kingdoms (See "Closer Look" 2:41–43), and Papal Rome. Deviating from this order causes the prophecies to lose harmony and creates great confusion. Some people attempt to interject Antiochus Epiphanes as the Little Horn power. This makes it impossible to understand what the prophecies represent. The beasts represented in these prophecies symbolize world powers. They are not individuals. Antiochus Epiphanes was not a world empire; he was one in a series of Selucid kings. The same "… Little Horn" appears in Daniel 7:21, 22, 26 and continues until the glorious Second Coming of Jesus. Antiochus Epiphanes was resting in his grave for about 164 years before the first coming of Christ. Furthermore, people today are familiar with the Grecian Empire and most are aware of the Persian Empire (Persian

Gulf), but few today would recognize Antiochus Epiphanes. If this power were greater than all the previous powers, it should be well known in history. However, most people need to find Antiochus Epiphanes in an encyclopedia to know who he was. On the other hand, most people are familiar with the Roman power—both church and state.

8:13, 14 The Length of the Vision

13. Then I heard a holy one speaking; and another holy one said to that certain one who was speaking, "How long will the vision be, concerning the daily sacrifices and the transgression of desolation, the giving of both the sanctuary and the host to be trampled underfoot?" 14. And he said to me, "For two thousand three hundred days; then the sanctuary shall be cleansed."

8:13, 14 TIME SET FOR JUDGMENT

Consider This

In chapter 7 Daniel saw the reign of the fourth beast and the coming up of the Little Horn. He had been shown as the Little Horn came to its end in 1798, that the judgment would start. In this chapter God is repeating and enlarging the picture. The Little Horn represents Pagan and Papal Rome. Pagan Rome destroyed the Temple at Jerusalem in A.D. 70 taking away the "… daily sacrifices" (8:13), and making the sanctuary "desolate." The question is asked, how long will this go on? And the answer is given, "… for 2,300 days" (8:14). The chapter ends without Daniel understanding the vision. In chapter 9, while Daniel is praying, the angel Gabriel comes again and explains the vision.

8:15, 16 The Angel Gabriel

15. Now it happened, when I, Daniel, had seen the vision and was seeking the meaning, that suddenly there stood before me one having the appearance of a man. 16. And I heard a man's voice between the banks of the Ulai, who called, and said, "Gabriel, make this man understand the vision."

8:17 Time of the End

17. So he came near where I stood, and when he came I was afraid and fell on my face; but he said to me, "Understand, son of man, that the vision refers to the time of the end."

8:17 TIME OF THE END

Consider This

The angel Gabriel tells Daniel that this vision concerns the "… Time of the End." This phrase will be used in chapters 11 and 12 to depict the period of time from 1798 until the Second Coming of Christ (See chapters 11:35; 12:4). God always has plans and orders events that are taking place. They move like clockwork, "… for at the appointed time the end shall be" (8:19).

8:18, 19 Touched By The Angel

18. Now, as he was speaking with me, I was in a deep sleep with my face to the ground; but he touched me, and stood me upright. 19. And he said, "Look, I am making known to you what shall happen in the latter time of the indignation; for at the appointed time the end shall be."

8:20–22 Interpretation of the Ram and Goat

20. "The ram which you saw, having the two horns—they are the kings of Media and Persia. 21. "And the male goat is the kingdom of Greece. The large horn that is between its eyes is the first king. Alexander 22. "As for the broken horn and the four that stood up in its place, four kingdoms shall arise out of that nation, but not with its power."

8:23–25 Little Horn Revealed

23. "And in the latter time of their kingdom, when the transgressors have reached their fullness, a king shall arise, having fierce features, who understands sinister schemes. 24. His power shall be mighty, but not by his own power; he shall destroy fearfully, and shall prosper and thrive; he shall destroy the mighty, and

also the holy people. 25. Through his cunning he shall cause deceit to prosper under his hand; and he shall magnify himself in his heart. He shall destroy many in their prosperity. He shall even rise against the Prince of princes; but he shall be broken without human hand."

8:23-25 PAGAN AND PAPAL ROME

Consider This

As the Grecian Empire slowly faded away, Pagan Rome attained the supremacy. "A king shall arise, having fierce features, who understands sinister schemes" (8:23). This description coincides with the picture of the fourth beast of Daniel 7, which represents Pagan Rome. Since Papal Rome was in many respects a continuation of the Roman Empire (Pagan Rome), there is a mingling of applications. Some of the points apply to both, while others apply to only one. The authority of the Roman Empire was utilized by both Pagan and Papal Rome; such as, through the crucifixion of Christ, and the persecution of Jewish and Christian people. Both Pagan and Papal Rome had "… destroyed the mighty and the holy people" (8:24). With Papal Rome taking over the power and authority of Pagan Rome, the texts says, "… but not by his own power" (8:24). Scripture enlarges on the Little Horn in Revelation 13. It reveals that this power of Papal Rome will continue until Christ returns. For then it will "… be broken without human hand" (8:25).

8:26, 27 Daniel's Sickness

26. "And the vision of the evenings and mornings which was told is true; therefore seal up the vision, for it refers to many days in the future." 27. And I, Daniel, fainted and was sick for days; afterward I arose and went about the king's business. I was astonished by the vision, but no one understood it.

8:26, 27 LATTER DAY VISION IMPORTANT

Consider This

This experience was so stressful for Daniel that he fainted and was sick. He didn't grasp the vision which Gabriel said was important. Daniel understood clearly who the Ram and Goat represented for he revealed this in verses 20, 21. However, he did not understand the 2,300 days of verse 14. Without question, Daniel had received all he could bear. Therefore, the angel said to seal it up, more was to be revealed in the next chapter.

Daniel prayed for understanding; how much more should we pray to comprehend this prophecy since we are closer to the last days than he was. The explanation is given in 9:24–27.

SUMMARY OF CHAPTER 8

As Daniel was permitted to look into the future, he saw Rome emerging in its three phases: the Roman Empire, the church of Rome, and the revival of the church/state union of the Roman power at the end of time. In verse 24 he saw this power at work during the Dark Ages as it attempted to extinguish the true worship of God by destroying, "… the mighty and also the holy people" (8:24). Verse 25 reveals, "… He shall destroy many in their prosperity" (8:25). The King James Version of the Bible says, "… and by peace shall destroy many." That is, its sudden reemergence to power will be disguised by a platform of *"peace"* . However, its true character has not changed and it will once again array its power against God and His people. He shall "…rise against the Prince of princes; but he shall be broken without human hand." (8:25), by Jesus Christ at His Second Coming.

Chapter 9

The Seventy-Week Prophecy

INSIDE THIS CHAPTER:

SUMMARY OF DANIEL CHAPTER 9

Closer Look

This is a continuation of the explanation of the vision relayed in Daniel chapter 8. The angel Gabriel had explained to Daniel the meaning of the beasts that he had seen. However, Daniel had been overcome and fainted before the entire explanation had been completed (8:27). The explanation for the time period referred to in 8:14, "For two thousand and three hundred days; then the sanctuary shall be cleansed," had not yet been revealed.

9:1–3 Prophecy Fulfilled

1. In the first year of Darius the son of Ahasuerus, of the lineage of the Medes, who was made king over the realm of the Chaldeans 2. in the first year of his reign I, Daniel understood by the books the number of the years specified by the word of the Lord, given through Jeremiah the prophet, that He would accomplish seventy years in the desolations of Jerusalem. 3. "Then I set my face toward the Lord God to make request by prayer and supplications, with fasting, sackcloth, and ashes."

9:4–17 Daniel's Prayer

4. And I prayed to the Lord my God, and made confession, and said, "O Lord, great and awesome God, who keeps His covenant and mercy with those who love Him, and with those who keep His commandments, 5. "We have sinned and committed iniquity, we have done wickedly and rebelled, even by departing from Your precepts and Your judgments. 6. "Neither have we heeded Your servants the prophets, who spoke in Your name to our kings and our princes, to our fathers and all the people of the land. 7. "O Lord, righteousness belongs to You, but to us shame of face, as it is this day—to the men of Judah, to the inhabitants of Jerusalem and all Israel, those near and those far off in all the countries to which You have driven them, because of the unfaithfulness which they have committed against You. 8. "O Lord, to us belongs shame of face, to our kings, our princes, and our fathers, because we have

sinned against You. 9. "To the Lord our God belong mercy and forgiveness, though we have rebelled against Him. 10. "We have not obeyed the voice of the Lord our God, to walk in His laws, which He set before us by His servants the prophets. 11. "Yes, all Israel has transgressed Your law, and has departed so as not to obey Your voice; therefore the curse and the oath written in the Law of Moses the servant of God have been poured out on us, because we have sinned against Him. 12. "And He has confirmed His words, which He spoke against us and against our judges who judged us, by bringing upon us a great disaster; for under the whole heaven such never has been done as what has been done to Jerusalem. 13. "As it is written in the Law of Moses, all this disaster has come upon us; yet we have not made our prayer before the Lord our God, that we might turn from our iniquities and understand Your truth. 14. Therefore the Lord has kept the disaster in mind, and brought it upon us; for the Lord our God is righteous in all the works which He does, though we have not obeyed His voice. 15. "And now, O Lord our God, who brought Your people out of the land of Egypt with a mighty hand, and made Yourself a name, as it is this day—we have sinned, we have done wickedly! 16. "O Lord, according to all Your righteousness, I pray, let Your anger and Your fury be turned away from Your city Jerusalem, Your holy mountain; because for our sins, and for the iniquities of our fathers, Jerusalem and Your people have become a reproach to all who are around us. 17. "Now therefore, our God, hear the prayer of Your servant, and his supplications, and for the Lord's sake cause Your face to shine on Your sanctuary, which is desolate."

9:14–17 DANIEL'S PRAYER

Consider This

No doubt Daniel had studied the promise of Jeremiah 18:6–10 and understood that the fulfillment of God's promises to the children of Israel were dependent upon their obedience to Him. Daniel was concerned that because of the lack of true repentance, God would lengthen their time of captivity and defer His promise to

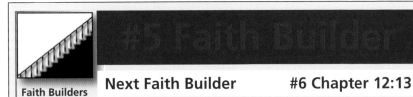

Faith Builders   **Next Faith Builder**   **#6 Chapter 12:13**

9:2, 3 COMPLETE TRUST

There are situations in the life of Daniel which give us indications of how he built his faith. Hebrews 11:6 says, "Without faith you cannot please God". The six examples in this book of how he built his faith are needed in today's hectic society.

Two elements through which faith works are Scripture and prayer. Daniel employed both in this ninth chapter. The reading of Scripture to the believer's spiritual nature is the same as food to his physical nature. "Man shall not live by bread alone, but by every word that proceeds from the mouth of God" (Matthew 4:4). One of the biggest reasons to study the Bible is to increase our faith. "So then faith comes by hearing, and hearing by the Word of God" (Romans 10:17). The reason we read God's Word is to give us faith. Daniel had read where Jeremiah prophesied that Israel would be in captivity for seventy years. The seventy years were coming to an end. By faith he knew that soon the children of Israel would be freed to go back to Jerusalem. Understanding the time and circumstances, Daniel sought his God in prayer. Prayer in the spiritual life of the Christian is the same as breathing is to the physical life. Prayer is the breath of the soul. But prayer has to be mixed with faith in order for it to accomplish its work. "And the prayer of faith will save the sick, and the Lord will raise him up. And if he has committed sins, he will be forgiven" (James 5:15). As Daniel mingled faith with his prayers, he could close his petition by saying, "O Lord, listen and act! Do not delay" (9:19). The promises in the Bible are sure. When we confess our sins and repent of them in faith, we can take hold of the assurances in His Word and know God will answer. In answer to Daniel's prayer, God sent an angel swiftly.

restore them to their homeland. In response, Daniel prayed one of the most outstanding prayers recorded in Scripture.

9:18, 19 Man's Righteousness

18. "O my God, incline Your ear and hear, open Your eyes and see our desolations, and the city which is called by Your name; for we do not present our supplications before You because of our righteous deeds, but because of Your great mercies. 19. "O Lord, hear! O Lord, forgive! O Lord, listen and act! Do not delay for Your own sake, my God, for Your city and Your people are called by Your name."

9:18, 19 MAN'S RIGHTEOUSNESS

Consider This

God does not play games or make deals; therefore, the righteousness of man could never be the basis upon which God would act. True, God calls upon us to live a holy life. God is holy and He wants us to be like Him. Our sins separate us from Him and bring a host of evil upon us. God's love and mercy do not fluctuate. Therefore, after Daniel had confessed his sins and the sins of Israel, all he could do was fall on the mercies of the Lord. "But God, who is rich in mercy, because of His great love with which He loved us" (Ephesians 2:4), did not disappoint his servant.

9:20–23 The Angel Gabriel Is Sent

20. Now while I was speaking, praying, and confessing my sin and the sin of my people Israel, and presenting my supplication before the Lord my God for the holy mountain of my God, 21. Yes, while I was speaking in prayer, the man Gabriel, whom I had seen in the vision at the beginning, being caused to fly swiftly, reached me about the time of the evening offering. 22. And he informed me, and talked with me, and said, "O Daniel, I have now come forth to give you skill to understand. 23. "At the beginning of your supplications the command went out, and I have come to tell you, for you are greatly beloved; therefore consider the matter, and understand the vision:

9:20–23 QUICK ANSWER TO PRAYER

Consider This

How fast do angels fly? Gabriel was standing beside God's throne when Daniel began his prayer. In about five minutes he was talking to Daniel. Gabriel flew swiftly indeed. We do not understand space travel! The purpose of Gabriel's visit was to help Daniel understand the vision he saw in 8:14. "And he said to me, 'For two thousand three hundred days; then the sanctuary shall be cleansed.'"

Compare the thought and wording of 8:16 in the instruction to Gabriel to, "… make this man to understand the vision …" with the thought and wording in 9:22, 23. Gabriel is preparing to consummate the instruction and deliver the key to understanding the time element of the prophecy. Since Gabriel had already explained all other aspects of the vision (8:20–25), the 2,300 days of 8:14 must be the subject about which he will give Daniel "… skill to understand" (9:22).

9:24–27 The Vision of the 2,300 Days Explained

24. "Seventy weeks are determined for your people and for your holy city, to finish the transgression, to make an end of sins, to make reconciliation for iniquity, to bring in everlasting righteousness, to seal up vision and prophecy, and to anoint the Most Holy. 25. "Know therefore and understand, that from the going forth of the command to restore and build Jerusalem until Messiah the Prince, there shall be seven weeks and sixty-two weeks; the street shall be built again, and the wall, even in troublesome times. 26. "And after the sixty-two weeks Messiah shall be cut off, but not for Himself; and the people of the prince who is to come shall destroy the city and the sanctuary. The end of it shall be with a flood, and till the end of the war desolations are determined, 27. Then he shall confirm a covenant with many for one week; but in the middle of the week He shall bring an end to sacrifice and offering. And on the wing of abominations shall

be one who makes desolate, even until the consummation, which is determined, is poured out on the desolate."

9:24–27A IRREFUTABLE PROOF OF THE MESSIAH

Closer Look

No agnostic, infidel, or atheist, has ever been able to disprove the prophecy recorded here in Daniel. This prediction will show that Jesus Christ is the Messiah, telling the very year He would begin His ministry and the time of His death. This prophecy has stood the test of time, so study it carefully. We must not forget in our study that Gabriel was explaining the 2,300 days to Daniel. The Jewish people had been in captivity for seventy years and the time had come for their deliverance. Uppermost in Daniel's mind was what was going to happen to them.

9:24–27B THE HOUR OF GOD'S JUDGMENT

Closer Look

The time had come for the children of Israel to go back to Jerusalem. God in His mercy granted to them a period of seventy weeks. Using the principle of a day representing one year (Ezekiel 4:6; Numbers 14:34), a period of 490 years was given to the Jewish people "… to make reconciliation for iniquity, to make an end of sins, and bring in everlasting righteousness" (9:24). The angel Gabriel tells Daniel to start counting when the decree is given for the Israelites to go back to Jerusalem. "Know therefore and understand, that from the going forth of the command to restore and build Jerusalem until Messiah the Prince, there shall be seven weeks and sixty-two weeks; the street shall be built again, and the wall, even in troublesome times" (9:25).

The command "… to restore and to build" (9:25), must restore both civil and religious government. Two previous decrees by Cyrus (Ezra 1:1-4) and Darius (Ezra 6:1-12) fell short of fulfilling these specifications. These gave the Jewish people the right to go back to Jerusalem, "… to build" (9:25), but not the right to be an independent nation, "to restore" (9:25). The decree of Artaxerxes in the seventh year of his reign, 457 B.C., was the first to completely fulfill the prophecy by giving them the right to have their own government.

The decree was given by King Artaxerxes in the fall of 457 B.C. (Ezra 7:12,13). From 457 B.C. it would be 69 weeks, or 483 years, until Messiah the Prince. Remember when you are working with B.C. dates you always subtract as you move down in time. The actual "… going forth" (9:25), of the command was in the autumn of 457 B.C. Subtracting 483 years from 457 B.C. takes you to the autumn of A.D. 27. You must take into account a zero year when you are going from B.C. dates to A.D. dates.

Luke 3 sheds light on the events that happened. Jesus was baptized by John the Baptist at the beginning of His ministry. Luke 3:23 states that Jesus was 30 years of age. Christian historians agree Christ was not born in A.D. 1, but in 4 B.C. due to an error in calculating His age.

Also in Luke 3:1 it says, "Now in the fifteenth year of the reign of Tiberius Caesar." According to secular history, the fifteenth year of Tiberius Caesar was A.D. 27, as prophesied when the 69 weeks, or 483 years, came to an end. Jesus began His ministry in A.D. 27, establishing without question that Jesus is the Messiah, the Savior of mankind.

Verse 26 of Daniel 9 leaves out the 7 weeks, or 49 years, which it took to rebuild the walls and city of Jerusalem, and counts from 408 B.C. to the baptism of Christ. Pagan Rome destroyed the city in A.D. 70. The angel told Daniel that 70 weeks, or 490 years, were given to his people. We have looked at 69 weeks, leaving one week to contemplate. The details of this last week are considered in verse 27. "Then He shall confirm a covenant with many for one week; but in the middle of the week He shall bring an end to sacrifices and offerings." The 70 weeks, or 490 years, ended in A.D. 34, so the last week would be the time from A.D. 27 to A.D. 34, a total of 7 years. In the middle of the week the sacrifices were to come to an end. 3½ years from A.D. 27, takes us to A.D. 31, the very year that the Lamb of God died and brought an end to the sacrificial system. Only Jesus Christ fulfills this prophecy. Both the Old and New Testaments testify to the fact of His Messiahship. (Isaiah 7:14; Luke 1:26, 27, 30, 31.) The Son of God died and salvation was secured for all mankind.

Adding 3½ years to A.D. 31 brings us to A.D. 34 and the end of the seventy weeks, or 490 years. The Jewish people had not done what God asked of them, and the gospel went to the Gentiles. The Scripture is clear that the Jewish people were to be a light to the Gentiles, but had failed in their responsibility.

Two events took place in Scripture that marked the carrying out of God's plan of taking the gospel to the Gentiles. Acts 9 records the conversion of Saul of Tarsus who said, "Then He said to me, 'Depart, for I will send you far from here to the Gentiles'" (Acts 22:21). The other event is in Acts 10. Peter was praying when he saw a sheet let down from heaven with unclean animals in it, and a voice said, "… Rise, Peter, kill and eat" (Acts 10:13), to which he responded by saying, "… Not so, Lord, for I have never eaten anything common or unclean" (Acts 10:14). Later at the home of a Roman soldier named Cornelius, Peter explained what the vision meant. "Then he said to them, 'You know how unlawful it is for a Jewish man to keep company with, or go to, one of another nation. But God has shown me that I should not call any man common or unclean" (Acts 10:28). The date of these occurrences was A.D. 34, at which time the gospel went to the Gentiles. This completes the last 3½ years of the week of 9:27.

We have now considered 490 years of the total 2,300 years given in Daniel 8:14. If we subtract 490 from 2,300 it leaves us 1810 years. Adding 1810 to A.D. 34 brings us to 1844 as the time of the cleansing of the sanctuary. The term "cleansing of the sanctuary" was also known in Scripture as "the Day of Atonement" or "the Day of Judgment". When Jesus returns, each case will have been decided, "And behold, I am coming quickly, and My reward is with Me, to give to every one according to his works" (Revelation 22:12). Judgment for the human race is going on in the courts of Heaven now. Each case is being investigated so that when Christ returns He will give life to those who have accepted and followed Him, and death to those whose names are not written in the Lamb's Book of Life.

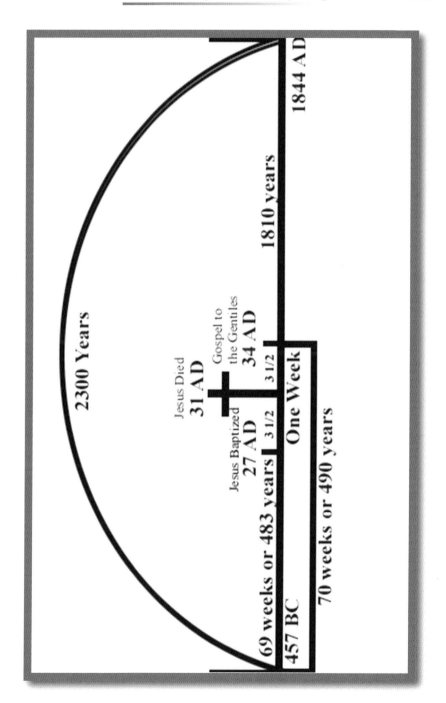

Chapter 10

Daniel's Vision of Christ

INSIDE THIS CHAPTER:

DANIEL'S FINAL PROPHECY CHAPTERS 10–12

Consider This

Chapters 10:5–12, 13 form the last prophecy of the book of Daniel. This prophecy follows the pattern of Repeat and Enlarge (See p. 69.). It covers much of the same ground as the rest of Daniel's visions. Then Daniel offers more detail on the antichrist, showing the ultimate victory of the Messiah whom chapter 9 pictures as being, "… cut off" (9:26). It then leads to and finishes with the Messiah's rescue of God's people.

It should be noted that this prophecy uses no prophetic symbolism such as beasts, horns, etc. There are also no figurative time references. This will become important as we study chapter 12.

Chapter 10 serves as an introduction to this final prophecy. Chapters 11:1–12:3 contain the prophecy itself. Chapter 12:4–13 is the summary or epilogue. Chapter 11 explains Middle Eastern history from Cyrus' time to that of Alexander the Great. It becomes more detailed as it deals with the powers that followed Alexander. Chapters 11 and 12 close with events that take place during the last days of earth's history.

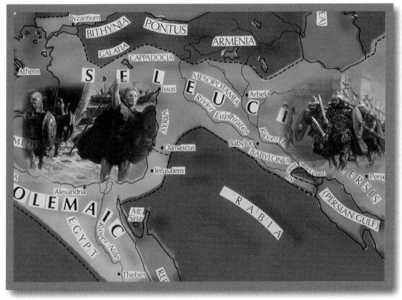

10:1–3 Daniel Fasting

1. In the third year of Cyrus king of Persia a message was revealed to Daniel, whose name was called Belteshazzar. The message was true, but the appointed time was long; and he understood the message, and had understanding of the vision. 2. In those days I, Daniel, was mourning three full weeks. 3. I ate no pleasant food, no meat or wine came into my mouth, nor did I anoint myself at all, till three whole weeks were fulfilled.

10:1–3 PRINCE OF PERSIA

Consider This

Daniel's fasting and mourning were because of the events affecting the Jewish people. At that time, opposition by the Samaritans against the Jews going back to Jerusalem was foremost on Daniel's mind. Zerubbabel had just returned from Jerusalem and given a report of the progress. There was a serious threat that Cyrus' decree for the children of Israel to return to Jerusalem and rebuild, might not be carried to completion because of the false reports sent by the Samaritans. For three weeks the angel Gabriel had grappled with the powers of darkness; trying to nullify the work of darkness on the mind of the Prince of Persia. Through this great conflict the victory was gained and the forces of evil were restrained during Cyrus' and his son, Cambyses', lifetimes.

10:4–9 Daniel's Vision of Christ

4. Now on the twenty-fourth day of the first month, as I was by the side of the great river, that is, the Tigris, 5. I lifted my eyes and looked, and behold, a certain man clothed in linen, whose waist was girded with gold of Uphaz! 6. His body was like beryl, his face like the appearance of lightning, his eyes like torches of fire, his arms and feet like burnished bronze in color, and the sound of his words like the voice of a multitude. 7. And I, Daniel, alone saw the vision, for the men who were with me did not see the vision; but a great terror fell upon them, so that they fled to hide themselves. 8. Therefore I was left alone when I saw this

great vision, and no strength remained in me; for my vigor was turned to frailty in me, and I retained no strength. 9. Yet I heard the sound of his words; and while I heard the sound of his words I was in a deep sleep on my face, with my face to the ground.

10:4–9 CHRIST THE LORD

Consider This

The vision Daniel had is almost identical to the description of Christ that John received in Revelation. "And in the midst of the seven lampstands One like the Son of Man, clothed with a garment down to the feet and girded about the chest with a golden band. His head and His hair were white like wool, as white as snow, and His eyes like a flame of fire; His feet were like fine brass, as if refined in a furnace, and His voice as the sound of many waters; He had in His right hand seven stars, out of His mouth went a sharp two-edged sword, and His countenance was like the sun shining in its strength" (Revelation 1:13–16).

It is interesting that the picture of Christ given by Daniel in 10:5, 6 was before He was born of Mary and took the nature of man. John's description in Revelation 1:13–16 is after His resurrection and ascension to Heaven. Both are similar except for the hair that John mentions, and His body like beryl that Daniel describes. The stone beryl is identified as topaz, chrysolite, chalcedony and carbuncle. It was very precious and was one of the stones in the high priest's breastplate (Exodus 28:20). It is used in the description of "… my beloved …" in Song of Solomon 5:14, in the description of Ezekiel's wheels (Ezekiel 1:16), and is the eighth foundation of the New Jerusalem (Revelation 21:20).

10:10–12 The Touch of An Angel

10. Then, suddenly, a hand touched me, which made me tremble on my knees and on the palms of my hands. 11. And he said to me, "O Daniel, man greatly beloved, understand the words that I speak to you, and stand upright, for I have now been sent to you."

While he was speaking this word to me, I stood trembling. 12. Then he said to me, "Do not fear, Daniel, for from the first day that you set your heart to understand, and to humble yourself before your God, your words were heard; and I have come because of your words.

10:13 Michael

13. "But the prince of the kingdom of Persia withstood me twenty-one days: and behold, Michael, one of the chief princes, came to help me, for I had been left alone there with the kings of Persia."

10:13 MICHAEL

Consider This

The word "Michael" is used in 10:13,21; 12:1; Jude 9; Revelation 12:7. In each case it is when the power of Heaven is in direct conflict with Satan. In Jude 9 Michael is called the Archangel, and it is the Archangel who will call the dead from their graves (1 Thessalonians 4:16). The word "Michael" in Hebrew means "who is like God".

10:14–17 Daniel Talks to "My Lord"

14. "Now I have come to make you understand what will happen to your people in the latter days, for the vision refers to many days yet to come." 15. When he had spoken such words to me, I turned my face toward the ground and became speechless. 16. And suddenly, one having the likeness of the sons of men touched my lips; then I opened my mouth and spoke, saying to him who stood before me, "My lord, because of the vision my sorrows have overwhelmed me, and I have retained no strength. 17. "For how can this servant of my lord talk with you, my lord? As for me, no strength remains in me now, nor is any breath left in me."

10:18–21 Strengthened by the Angel

18. Then again the one having the likeness of a man touched me and strengthened me. 19. And he said, "O man greatly beloved, fear not! Peace be to you; be strong, yes, be strong!" So when he spoke

to me I was strengthened, and said, "Let my lord speak, for you have strengthened me," 20. Then he said, "Do you know why I have come to you? And now I must return to fight with the prince of Persia; and when I have gone forth, indeed the prince of Greece will come. 21. "But I will tell you what is noted in the Scripture of Truth. (No one upholds me against these, except Michael your prince.

10:20 PRINCE OF PERSIA AND PRINCE OF GREECE

Consider This

Nations rise and fall at the hand of God. The angel of God told Daniel that he was going back to continue wrestling with the power of darkness for the mind of the King of Persia. As long as the angel of God held back the winds of strife the empire of Persia existed. As the Scripture points out, "… and when I have gone forth" (10:20), the prince of Greece (Alexander the Great) invaded the Persian Empire and it soon passed into history.

Chapter 11

Warring Kings of the North and South

INSIDE THIS CHAPTER:

OUTLINE FOR CHAPTER 11

Closer Look

❖ (1–2) Babylon has fallen and the Medo-Persian Empire comes to an end.

❖ (3–13) The rise of Greece under Alexander the Great and the four divisions of his empire.

❖ (14–30) The rise of the Pagan Roman Empire.

❖ (31–35) The Church of the Dark Ages and the development of Papal Rome.

❖ (36–39) The rise of Atheism.

❖ (40–45) The reestablishment of Papal Rome and a description of last day events leading to the climax of human history and the Second Coming of Jesus.

11:1, 2 Medo-Persia

1. Also in the first year of Darius the Mede, I, even I, stood up to confirm and strengthen him.) 2. "And now I will tell you the truth: behold three more kings will arise in Persia, and the fourth shall be far richer than them all; by his strength, through his riches, he shall stir up all against the realm of Greece."

11:1, 2 RULE OF MEDO-PERSIA

Closer Look

What Gabriel is telling Daniel in the last verse of chapter 10 is continued in chapter 11, verse 1. The four kings that followed Darius were Cambyses, Gaumata, Darius I and Xerses, also known as Ahasuerus, of the book of Esther. Ahasuerus was proud of his wealth and position, and attacked the Greek city-states. They united and saved their freedom.

11:3, 4 Greece

3. "Then a mighty king shall arise, who shall rule with great dominion, and do according to his will. 4. "And when he has arisen, his kingdom shall be broken up and divided toward the four winds of heaven, but not among his posterity nor according

to his dominion with which he ruled, for his kingdom shall be uprooted, even for others besides these.

11:3, 4 DOMINION OF GREECE

Closer Look

Alexander the Great's dominion was the largest empire the world had known at that time. This monarch who ruled from the Adriatic to India had hardly reached the height of his power when suddenly he fell ill; eleven days later he was dead, leaving no one in his immediate family to take control of the country. Finally, through a confederation of four generals, Alexander's domain was divided into four kingdoms, representing the same division as the four heads on the leopard in 7:6, and the four horns on the goat in 8:8.

11:5 King of the South

5. "Then the king of the South shall become strong, as well as one of his princes; and he shall gain power over him and have dominion. His dominion shall be a great dominion."

11:6 King of the North

6. "And at the end of some years they shall join forces, for the daughter of the king of the South shall go to the king of the North to make an agreement: but she shall not retain the power of her authority, and neither he nor his authority shall stand; but she shall be given up, with those who brought her, and with him who begot her, and with him who strengthened her in those times."

11:5, 6 KING OF THE SOUTH AND KING OF THE NORTH

Key to Prophecy

Throughout this chapter the King of the South and the King of the North will be referred to many times. The easiest way to understand these terms is to look at the geography. Daniel has been praying about his people and their going back to Jerusalem. With Jerusalem being the center, the nations to the north are referred to as "King of the North" and from time to time different ones became dominant, such as Greece, Syria and Rome. Also the nations lying south of Jerusalem are mentioned as "King of the South". The most prominent would be Egypt. Egypt plays a major role in this chapter until about 31 B.C., when she was overthrown by Rome. Since that time Egypt has never been a literal dominant force.

The Scripture speaks of Spiritual Egypt (Revelation 11:8), because of her opposition to God's people, and Pharaoh's statement, "Who is the Lord, that I should obey His voice to let Israel go? I do not know the Lord, nor will I let Israel go" (Exodus 5:2). Unlike the "King of the North", the "King of the South" remains constant. After 31 B.C. it represents the atheistic power of Egypt that lay to the south of Jerusalem.

This chapter shows God's people being attacked by false religion from the north and atheistic beliefs from the south. The angel Gabriel told Daniel that the vision he was shown, concerning his people, would extend until the latter days (10:14). Since the vision is going to take us down through time, God's people (Israel) will refer to the Jews until A.D. 31. After their rejection of the Messiah in A.D. 31, the term will refer to God's people. In verses 36–40 of chapter 11 the "King of the South" appears again, this time not as (literal) Egypt, but as a power which will be against God's people in the last days and will destroy many (spiritual Egypt).

"King of the North" is the primary term used in Daniel 11. The north is where the rain was and the land was green, fertile, and desirable. The devil, being in opposition to God, said he would place his throne in the north. "For you have said in your heart: I will ascend into heaven, I will exalt my throne above the stars of God: I will also sit on the mount of the congregation on the farthest sides of the north" (Isaiah 14:13). The land lying north of Jerusalem included such nations as Babylon, Greece, Syria and Rome, depending upon the time in history the Scripture is talking about. Each of these kingdoms would oppose the followers of God.

Jeremiah prophesied that Babylon would come out of the north, "Behold I will send and take all the families of the north, says the Lord, and Nebuchadnezzar, the king of Babylon, My servant, and will bring them against this land, against its inhabitants, and against these nations all around" (Jeremiah 25:9). Today Babylon lies in ruins but the New Testament talks about Spiritual Babylon. "And on her forehead a name was written: Mystery, Babylon the Great, the Mother of Harlots and of the Abominations of the Earth" (Revelation 17:5). As you progress through chapter 11 of Daniel, you will see these powers in opposition to one another and both hindering the cause of God upon the earth. With the breaking up of the Grecian Empire, two powers arise — Egypt in the south and Syria in the north. Daniel will describe the interchange between these two kingdoms.

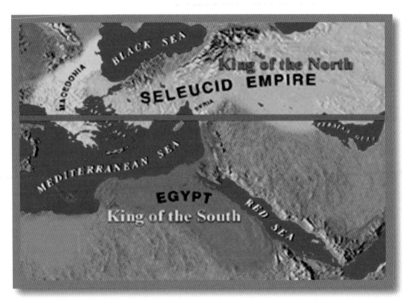

11:7–14 Egypt and Syria

7. "But from a branch of her roots one shall arise in his place, who shall come with an army, enter the fortress of the king of the North, and deal with them and prevail. 8. "And he shall also carry

their gods captive to Egypt, with their princes and their precious articles of silver and gold; and he shall continue more years than the king of the North. 9. "Also the king of the North shall come to the kingdom of the king of the South, but shall return to his own land. 10. "However his sons shall stir up strife, and assemble a multitude of great forces; and one shall certainly come and overwhelm and pass through; then he shall return to his fortress and stir up strife. 11. "And the king of the South shall be moved with rage, and go out and fight with him, with the king of the North, who shall muster a great multitude; but the multitude, shall be given into the hand of his enemy. 12. "When he has taken away the multitude his heart will be lifted up; and he will cast down tens of thousands, but he will not prevail. 13. "For the king of the North will return and muster a multitude greater than the former, and shall certainly come at the end of some years with a great army and much equipment. 14. "And in those times many shall rise up against the king of the South; also certain violent men of your people shall exalt themselves in fulfillment of the vision, but they shall fall."

11:7–14 CONFLICTS OF THE KINGS OF NORTH AND SOUTH

Closer Look

As the Grecian Empire declined, two dominant powers arose: Egypt to the south and one of Alexander's generals, Seleucus, to the north. Seleucus placed himself under the king of Egypt, Ptolemy. "… as well as one of his princes; and he shall gain power over him and have dominion" (11:5). Later he succeeded and took over the territories in Mesopotamia and became stronger than Ptolemy. His kingdom extended from Hellespont to northern India. Therefore he became the king of the North. "… His dominion shall be a great dominion" (11:5).

Trying to bring peace between the two nations, Antiochus II, the grandson of Seleucus, married Bernice, the daughter of Ptolemy II, king of Egypt. "And at the end of some years they shall join forces, for the daughter of the king of the South shall go to the king of the North to make an agreement" (11:6). Also, Antiochus II expelled his former wife, Laodice. After a son was born to Bernice and Antiochus II, Laodice and Antiochus II were able to patch up their differences, or so the king thought. But Laodice had Bernice and her infant son killed, plus all her servants, and then poisoned Antiochus II. "But she shall not retain the power of her authority, and neither he nor his authority shall stand; but she shall be given up, with those who brought her, and with him who begot her, and with him who strengthened her in those times" (11:6).

Ptolemy III, the brother of Bernice, invaded Syria and overthrew it, avenging his sister's death. "But from a branch of her roots one shall arise in his place, who shall come with an army, enter the fortress of the king of the North, and deal with them and prevail. And he shall also carry their gods captive to Egypt, with their princes and their precious articles of silver and gold; and he shall continue more years than the king of the North" (11:7, 8).

After numerous battles between the two powers, Antiochus III, King of the North, and Ptolemy IV, King of the South, met at the battle of Raphia (217 B.C.). Ptolemy IV was victorious but did not follow through, and sixteen years later Antiochus III avenged himself and defeated Egypt. "And the king of the South shall be moved with rage, and go out and fight with him, with the king of the North, who shall muster a great multitude; but the multitude shall be given into the hand of his enemy. When he has taken away the multitude, his heart will be lifted up: and he will cast down tens of thousands, but he will not prevail. For the king of the North will return and muster a multitude greater than the former, and shall certainly come at the end of some years with a great army and much equipment" (11:11–13).

On the scene of action now was rising a new power, small to begin with, but beginning to show its muscle. In fact, it was during the reign of Antiochus III that the new contenders for world domination, the Romans, decided to have a say in the affairs of Syria and Egypt. "And in those times many shall rise up against the king of the South; also certain violent men of your people shall exalt themselves in fulfillment of the vision, but they shall fall" (11:14).

11:15–30 Pagan Rome

15. "So the king of the North shall come and build a siege mound, and take a fortified city; and the forces of the South shall not withstand him. Even his choice troops shall have no strength to resist. 16. "But he who comes against him shall do according to his own will, and no one shall stand against him. He shall stand in the Glorious Land with destruction in his power. 17. "He shall also set his face to enter with the strength of his whole kingdom, and upright ones with him; thus shall he do. And he shall give him the daughter of women to destroy it; but she shall not stand with him, or be for him. 18. "After this he shall turn his face to the coastlands, and shall take many. But a ruler shall bring the reproach against them to an end; and with the reproach removed, he shall turn back on him. 19. "Then he shall turn his face toward the fortress of his own land; but he shall stumble and fall, and not be found. 20. "There shall arise in his place one who imposes taxes on the glorious kingdom; but within a few days he shall be destroyed, but not in anger or in battle. 21. "And in his place shall arise a vile person, to whom they will not give the honor of royalty; but he shall come in peaceably, and seize the kingdom by intrigue. 22. "With the force of a flood they shall be swept away from before him and be broken, and also the prince of the covenant. 23. "And after the league is made with him he shall act deceitfully, for he shall come up and become strong with a small number of people. 24. "He shall enter peaceably, even into the richest places of the province; and he shall do what his fathers have not done, nor his forefathers: he shall disperse among them the plunder, spoil, and riches; and he shall devise his plans against the strongholds, but only for a time. 25. "He shall stir up his power

and his courage against the king of the South with a great army. And the king of the South shall be stirred up to battle with a very great and mighty army; but he shall not stand, for they shall devise plans against him. 26. "Yes, those who eat of the portion of his delicacies shall destroy him, his army shall be swept away, and many shall fall down slain. 27. "Both these kings' hearts shall be bent on evil, and they shall speak lies at the same table; but it shall not prosper, for the end will still be at the appointed time. 28. "While returning to his land with great riches, his heart shall be moved against the holy covenant; so he shall do damage and return to his own land. 29. "At the appointed time he shall return and go toward the south; but it shall not be like the former or the latter. 30. "For ships from Cyprus shall come against him; therefore he shall be grieved, and return in rage against the holy covenant, and do damage. So he shall return and show regard for those who forsake the holy covenant."

11:15–30 RULE OF PAGAN ROME

Closer Look

The northern territory had been controlled by Syria. A new force was now rising that was destined to become the king of the North. In 63 B.C. the Roman invasion of Palestine took place. "So the king of the North shall come and build a siege mound, and take a fortified city; and the forces of the South shall not withstand him. Even his choice troops shall have no strength to resist. "But he who comes against him shall do according to his own will, and no one shall stand against him. He shall stand in the Glorious Land with destruction in his power" (11:15, 16).

Rome was beginning to exercise her strength when Ptolemy XI, king of Egypt, died in 51 B.C. He placed his two children, Cleopatra and Ptolemy XII, under the guardianship of Rome. Just three years later Cleopatra became the mistress of Julius Caesar. Verses 17–20 tell how Julius Caesar took his campaign to the coastlands and was assassinated in 44 B.C. Cleopatra didn't stand with Caesar, but turned her affections to Mark Anthony. "He shall also set his face to enter with the strength of his whole kingdom, and upright ones with him; thus shall he do. And he shall give him the daughter of women to destroy it; but she shall not stand with him, or be for him. After this he shall turn his face to the coastlands, and shall take many. But a ruler shall bring the reproach against them to an end; and with the reproach removed, he shall turn back on him. Then he shall turn his face toward the fortress of his own land; but he shall stumble and fall, and not be found" (11:17–19).

Caesar Augustus, who succeeded Julius Caesar, was the one who established the Roman Empire. "There shall arise in his place one who imposes taxes on the glorious kingdom; but within a few days he shall be destroyed, but not in anger or in battle" (11:20). "And it came to pass in those days that a decree went out from Caesar Augustus that all the world should be taxed" (Luke 2:1).

Augustus the King of the North and Anthony the King of the South, fought in the battle of Actium. Cleopatra, who could not be depended upon, was frightened by the din of battle and withdrew, taking with her the sixty ships supplied by the Egyptian navy. Anthony followed her and thereby conceded the victory to Augustus. His supporters went over to Augustus. Finally, he committed suicide.

Augustus reigned for more than 40 years and died peacefully in bed in A.D. 14. He was succeeded by his adopted son, Tiberius, who was eccentric, misunderstood, unloved, and ruling at the time the "Prince of the Covenant", Jesus Christ, was put to death. "And in his place shall arise a vile person, to whom they will not give the honor of royalty; but he shall come in peaceably, and seize the kingdom by intrigue. With force of a flood they shall be swept away from before him and be broken, and also the prince of the covenant" (11:21, 22).

Rome continued her conquest of the world, bringing Judea into submission, and destroying Jerusalem in A.D. 70. Rome was to rule longer than any other power up to that time—from 168 B.C. to A.D. 476. "And after the league is made with him he shall act deceitfully, for he shall come up and become strong with a small number of people" (11:23). Imperial Rome made treaties with other nations to protect and promote mutual interest. Rome assumed the role of friend and protector, only to "… work deceitfully" (11:23), by turning their agreements to her own advantage. She often imposed the burdens of conquest on her "allies", but usually reserved the rewards of conquest for herself. Eventually these "allies" were absorbed into the Roman Empire. "… for a time" (11:24)—a considerable period of time, in fact—no "… strongholds" (11:24), were able to withstand the determined pressure of the invincible legion of Rome.

The Roman Empire rose to prominence and brought all of her enemies under her foot. Great persecution was inflicted on the Christians and ended with Diocletion. Their (the Roman Empire) "… hearts shall be bent on evil" (11:27).

With the supposed conversion of Constantine the persecution stopped. That which had been an affliction to the church had also kept it pure. Now, worse than their suffering, Constantine brought the world into the church. "His heart shall be moved against the holy covenant; so he shall do damage and return to his own land" (11:28). That Holy Covenant is the plan of salvation. It was made in the beginning and sealed by the death of Christ. Rome is the power referred to here and Constantine opened a floodgate of opposition to the plan of salvation for the lives of men and women:

1. He marched his army through the river and told them they had all been baptized and were now Christians.
2. He took pagan ceremonies and incorporated them into the Christian Church.
3. He signed the Edict of Constantine in A.D. 321 announcing that the pagan day of worshipping the sun would take the place of the Lord's Sabbath (See Mark 2:28; Matthew 12:8; Luke 6:5).

These actions brought great damage to the church, "… but it shall not be like the former or the latter" (11:29).

Constantine's effort to revive the Roman Empire to its "… former" (11:29) glory and power was not successful and the moving of the capital to Constantinople began the downfall of the Roman Empire. "Both these kings' hearts shall be bent on evil, and they shall speak lies at the same table; but it shall not prosper, for the end will still be at the appointed time. While returning to his land with great riches, his heart shall be moved against the holy covenant; so he shall do damage and return to his own land. At the appointed time he shall return and go toward the south; but it shall not be like the former or the latter" (11:27–29).

Barbarian tribes, called the Goths, were invading the Roman Empire and breaking it into pieces. These Germanic tribes became the nations of Western Europe that are mentioned in chapters 2 and 7.

Verse 30 speaks of one of the Barbarian tribes from Cyprus sailing against Rome. The Vandals, actually sailed their ships into the Roman fleet and set them on fire. This destroyed nearly every Roman ship, thus hastening the demise of the empire. Rome was certainly grieved as the text indicates, "… he shall be grieved" (11:30). (Because of the unspeakable deeds perpetrated against Rome by this Barbarian tribe, individuals involved in malicious destruction are to this day called "vandals" and their acts are referred to as "vandalism".)

"For ships from Cyprus shall come against him; therefore, he shall be grieved and return in rage against the holy covenant, and do damage. So he shall return and show regard for those who forsake the holy covenant" (11:30).

11:31–35 Papal Rome
31. "And forces shall be mustered by him, and they shall defile the sanctuary fortress, then they shall take away the daily sacrifices,

and place there the abomination of desolation. 32. "Those who do wickedly against the covenant he shall corrupt with flattery; but the people who know their God shall be strong, and carry out great exploits. 33. "And those of the people who understand shall instruct many; yet for many days they shall fall by sword and flame, by captivity and plundering. 34. "Now when they fall, they shall be aided with a little help; but many shall join with them by intrigue. 35. "And some of those of understanding shall fall, to refine them, purge them, and make them white, until the time of the end; because it is still for the appointed time."

11:31–35 THE RISE OF PAPAL ROME

Closer Look

Verses 31–35 place the Papal Power in control. With its last serious opposition eliminated (Ostrogoths A.D. 538), the Papacy showed her crushing power. "… and force shall be mustered by him" (11:31). With the Papal Power now in control and the arms of state at their command, persecution followed.

However, Daniel gives a note of hope with the words "… but the people that do know their God shall be strong and carry out great exploits" (11:32). Throughout the Dark Ages, God always had faithful followers who would stand firmly for the truth. This was a period of frightful persecution. "… yet for many days they shall fall by the sword, and by flame, by captivity, and by spoil" (11:33). It was a time when the fires of persecution burned hot and millions of God's faithful went to a martyr's death.

Little help was given during the Dark Ages. This was a time of great physical and spiritual testing. According to the text many of God's saints would be "purified" and made "white" by persecution "… even to the Time of the End" (11:35).

11:35 TIME OF THE END

Key to Prophecy

The term "… Time of the End" (11:35), is used here for the first time, but Daniel will use the phrase several times after this. Daniel 7 says that the Little Horn would rule for a "… time, times and a half of time" (7:25), ending in 1798. Daniel 11 says that God's people will suffer until the "… Time of the End." On February 10, 1798, Napoleon's general Berthier marched into Rome and took the Pope prisoner, ending the time of persecution and the Papacy as a world power. This began what Daniel referred to as the "… Time of the End." Hereafter the term "Time of the End" will refer to the time from 1798 until the Second Coming of Christ. Daniel says "… it is still for the appointed time" (11:35). To have a clear understanding of the following verses and the details of prophecy for the last days, 1798 must be remembered as the "… appointed time" (11:35), by God and referred to in the Bible as the beginning of the "Time of the End". Earth's inhabitants have been living in the "Time of the End" since 1798. It must now be nearing the "end of time". The "King of the North" at this time referred to Papal Rome. She came to an end as a world power in 1798. She will rise again as described in the last verses of chapter 11.

11:36–39 Atheism

36. "Then the king shall do according to his own will: he shall exalt and magnify himself above every god, shall speak blasphemies against the God of gods, and shall prosper till the wrath has been accomplished; for what has been determined shall be done. 37. "He shall regard neither the God of his fathers nor the desire of women, nor regard any god; for he shall magnify himself above them all. 38. "But in their place he shall honor a god of fortresses; and a god which his fathers did not know he shall honor with gold and silver, with precious stones and pleasant things. 39. "Thus he shall act against the strongest fortresses with a foreign god, which he shall acknowledge, and advance its glory; and he shall cause them to rule over many, and divide the land for gain."

11:36–39 A NEW GOD

Closer Look

"At the Time of the End the king of the South shall attack him," (11:40.) At this point it is very crucial to understand that "… the king of the South…" refers to Spiritual Egypt (See "Key to Prophecy" 11:5, 6; pp. 124, 125).

Because of Papal suppression, the nation of France threw off all belief in God and established the "Age of Reason", "… a god which his fathers did not know" (11:38). On November 26, 1793, she issued a decree abolishing religion. The Papal Power, who had been foremost in persecuting "… by the sword and flame, by captivity and plundering" (11:33), was now the object of attack. Thousands died by the guillotine. They threw the Bibles into the street and "… spoke blasphemies against the God of gods" (11:36). The King of the South (Spiritual Egypt), who had been quiet, suddenly arose. It was the Pharaoh of Egypt, the King of the South, who had said, "Who is the Lord, that I should obey His voice to let Israel go? I do not know the Lord, nor will I let Israel go" (Exodus 5:2).

Now atheism (Spiritual Egypt) had risen to power. Napoleon, wanting to turn Europe into one nation, realized that it could not be done without overthrowing the Papal power; thus the King of the South sent his general, Berthier, into Rome on February 10, 1798, and took the Pope, the King of the North, captive.

Out of the rise of atheism in France came movements that would war against the God of Heaven. George Hegel, 1797, the father of atheism, in philosophy and theology, introduced higher criticism of Scripture. Charles Darwin, 1837, brought in evolution of the species, turning man from his Creator. Karl Marx, 1843, introduced Communistic atheism, which took away the land of the people and gave it to the state, "… and divide the land for gain" (11:39). Sigmund Freud, 1873, psychoanalyst, taught the loss of morals and turned many from, "… the desire of women" (11:37).

11:40–45 Papal Power Re-established
40. "At the Time of the End the king of the South shall attack him, and the king of the North shall come against him like a whirlwind, with chariots, horsemen, and with many ships; and he shall enter the countries, overwhelm them, and pass through.

41. "He shall also enter the Glorious Land, and many countries shall be overthrown : but these shall escape from his hand Edom, Moab, and the prominent people of Ammon. 42. "He shall stretch out his hand against the countries, and the land of Egypt shall not escape. 43. "He shall have power over the treasures of gold and silver, and over all the precious things of Egypt; also the Libyans and Ethiopians shall follow at his heels. 44. "But news from the east and the north shall trouble him; therefore he shall go out with great fury to destroy and annihilate many. 45. "And he shall plant the tents of his palace between the seas and the glorious holy mountain; yet he shall come to his end, and no one will help him."

11:40–45 KING OF THE NORTH RISES TO POWER

Closer Look

"… And the king of the North shall come against him like a whirlwind, with chariots, horsemen, and with many ships; and he shall enter the countries, overwhelm them, and pass through" (11:40). Quickly, almost before they realized it, Atheistic Communism fell. *Time* magazine February 24, 1992, in an article entitled "Holy Alliance" tells how the Papal Power ("… the king of the North"), was foremost in bringing an end to Atheistic Communism ("… the king of the South"). "Only President Ronald Reagan and Pope John Paul II were present in the Vatican Library on Monday, June 7, 1992. It was the first time the two had met, and they talked for 50 minutes... . In that meeting, Reagan and the Pope agreed to undertake a clandestine campaign to hasten the dissolution of the communist empire...". 'Nobody believed the collapse of communism would happen this fast or on this timetable,' says a cardinal who is one of the Pope's closest aides." In December, 1990, communism fell in Poland, and as the Scripture said, "… like a whirlwind" (11:40), the other communistic nations fell in 1991.

A new power had arisen, as reported in the Toronto Star, March 9, 1992 in an article by Mikhail Gorbachev. "Now it can be said that everything which took place in Eastern Europe in recent years would have been impossible without the Pope's efforts and the enormous role, including the political role, which he played in the world arena. Pope John Paul II will play an enormous political role now that profound changes have occurred in European history."

"He shall also enter the Glorious Land, and many countries shall be overthrown: but these shall escape from his hand Edom, Moab, and the prominent people of Ammon" (11:41). The Edomites, Moabites, and the people of Ammon were once Israelites, but became Israel's fiercest opponents. Esau's descendants became the Edomites. Moab and Ben-ammi were the sons of Lot by his two daughters (Gen. 19:36-38). Their descendants became the Moabites and the people of Ammon, which represent the Muslim world today.

Although it seems that the Muslim world escaped the hand of the Papal power. "He shall stretch out his hand against the countries, ...and the Libyans and the Ethiopians shall follow at his heels" (11:42, 43.) In ancient times, Libyans and the Ethiopians were considered to be the furthermost reaches of the then known world. Near the end of time "all nations" will follow him and no one will escape. "... and all the world marveled and followed the beast" (Revelation 13:3).

"But news from the east and the north shall trouble him; therefore he shall go out with great fury to destroy and annihilate many." (11:44.) The details of this verse are yet future and they picture a sudden turn of events. At the height of Papal support he will go out to destroy God's people. We realize that we are living in the closing hours of earth's history. We should be alert to the events that are taking place in the world today. Daniel said the Papal Power would increase through the final years of the "... Time of the End" (11:35), but this will not last. "... yet he shall come to his end and no one will help him" (11:45). Then Jesus Christ will come again.

Second Coming

Chapter 12

Prophecy of the End Time

INSIDE THIS CHAPTER:

Introduction to Chapter 12

Consider This

Please reread the "Consider This" at the beginning of chapter 10. This will explain the significance chapter 12 plays in Daniel's final message given in chapters 10–12.

"TIME" IN BIBLE PROPHECY

Key to Prophecy

Time in Bible prophecy can be either literal or figurative. Jeremiah prophesied the 70-year captivity of his people literally (See Jeremiah 25:12).

When a prophecy is figurative or symbolic, it will use beasts, horns, crowns, etc., to represent something else. The time represented will be figurative or symbolic also. Examples would be:

Daniel 7 – where nations and powers are depicted as beasts with wings and horns, etc.

Daniel 8 – also depicts nations and powers as beasts and horns and speaks of 2,300 days which represent 2,300 years.

Revelation 12:14 – pictures the church as a woman with eagle's wings flying into the wilderness for a time, times and a half time (See "Closer Look" 7:23–25 for an explanation of a time, times and a half time).

Starting with chapter 10 there are no symbols or beasts.

12:1–3 End of Time

1. "At that time Michael shall stand up, the great Prince who stands watch over the sons of your people; and there shall be a time of trouble, such as never was since there was a nation, even to that time. And at that time your people shall be delivered, every one who is found written in the book. 2. And many of those who sleep in the dust of the earth shall awake, some to everlasting life, some to shame and everlasting contempt. 3. Those who are wise

shall shine like the brightness of the firmament, and those who turn many to righteousness like the stars forever and ever."

12:1–3 PROBATION CLOSES FOR MANKIND

Closer Look

For a clearer understanding, when the Scriptures were being divided into chapters and verses, chapter 11 should have continued to chapter 12, verse 3. The dividing of Scripture into chapters and verses took place long after the Bible was written and was not inspired. The standing up of Michael (Christ ends His work as man's intercessor in the courts of Heaven), the period of tribulation (the beginning of the time of trouble on earth), and the raising of the dead take place "… at that time" (12:1), that is, when the great persecution and the power described in chapter 11:40–45 is coming to its end. These events do not occur immediately. They occur within a brief time period. Beginning with verse 4, Daniel is given a more detailed view of these closing events on earth and the beginning of the everlasting kingdom of God.

12:4 Sealing of the Book

4. "But you, Daniel, shut up the words, and seal the book until the Time of the End; many shall run to and fro, and knowledge shall increase."

12:4 THE BOOK SEALED

Closer Look

In other words, the angel explained that the events Daniel saw in vision needed to be "… shut up" (12:4), and the book, "… sealed" (12:4). Men will run "… to and fro" (12:4), trying to understand, but God promised that, "… knowledge shall increase" (12:4), and this prophecy will be understood at "… the Time of the End" (12:4). The phrase "… Time of the End" (12:4) refers to a period of time beginning in 1798, continuing until the Second

Coming of Christ (See "Key to Prophecy" 11:35, Time of the End, for more details).

12:5, 6 Daniel's Final Question

5. Then I, Daniel, looked; and there stood two others, one on this riverbank and the other on that riverbank. 6. And one said to

the man clothed in linen, who was above the waters of the river, "How long shall the fulfillment of these wonders be?"

12:5, 6 DANIEL'S FINAL QUESTION

Closer Look

The fact that Daniel doesn't give a detailed description of the "… man clothed in linen" (12:5) or of the "… waters of the river" (12:5) leads us to believe that this is a question about Daniel's final prophecy that started in chapter 10. It could be said that verse 5 begins God's epilogue or final instructions to Daniel. The term "… wonders" (12:5) therefore, refers to the events mentioned in chapter 12:1-3 (the time of trouble, the Second Coming of Christ, the resurrection of the righteous and the deliverance of the saints).

12:7–13 ANSWER TO DANIEL'S QUESTION

Key to Prophecy

Here this chapter becomes more difficult to understand. Many people have struggled to make it fit the previously discussed time prophecies that are given in the books of Daniel and Revelation. Bible students hold two plausible explanations that could fit the time descriptions God gave Daniel in His final message in verses 7–13. These two explanations hinge on the student's interpretation of the term "… daily" (12:11).

One explanation is that "… daily" (12:11) refers to paganism and that both Daniel 7:25 and 12:7 use the term, "time, times and a half of time", to represent the 1,260 years of papal supremacy which ended in 1798. Therefore, the 1,290 years mentioned in verse 11 had to end in 1798. Subtracting 1,290 from 1798 we arrive at A.D. 508.

Clovis the king of the Franks was converted to the Catholic faith and the Goths were overthrown in A.D. 508. The establishment of the Catholic Church and its supremacy in the West was set up at this point. This view holds that this final prophecy doesn't go beyond the "...Time of the End" (12:4), or in other words 1798.

Verse 12; however, makes an exception. Notice the words of the angel. "Blessed is he who waits, and comes to the one thousand three hundred and thirty-five days" (12:12). "… Waits, and comes to" (12:12), implies that the time would go beyond the date of 1798. Adding 1335 to the date of 508 that was established in verse 11 takes us to 1843. The great awakening of the Millerite movement known as the Midnight Cry began at that time. It announced the beginning of the investigative judgment in Heaven discussed in chapters 8 and 9.

The second explanation and the one that this author believes is more plausible holds that "… daily" (12:11) is Christ's mediatoral work in the Heavenly Sanctuary. Michael is speaking directly about the "… Time of the End" (12:4). He is saying that in this time of the end there will be a repeat performance of what happened through the Christian centuries except the time mentioned would be in literal years. The remainder of this book is devoted to this explanation.

12:7, 8 Man In Linen Answers

7. Then I heard the man clothed in linen, who was above the waters of the river, when he held up his right hand and his left hand to heaven, and swore by Him who lives forever, that it shall be for a time, times and half a time; and when the power of the holy people has been completely shattered, all these things shall be finished. 8. Although I heard, I did not understand. Then I said, "My lord, what shall be the end of these things?"

12:7, 8 MAN IN LINEN ANSWERS

Closer Look

Daniel did not understand what the angel was saying and asked the question, "What shall be the end of these things?" (12:7). He cannot be saying that he did not understand the "time, times, and half a time" referred to in chapter 7, for he understood this prophecy. "… and he understood the message, and had understanding of the vision" (10:1).

The angel put the second "… time, times, and a half time" (12:7) (or 1260 days) in a different time context which Daniel did not understand; however, he was given the assurance that it would be understood during the "… Time of the End" (12:4), or after 1798. This is one of the things that makes this part of Daniel 12 so difficult to understand. Even Daniel did not understand.

"When the power of the holy people has been completely shattered" (12:7), refers to the time of the latter rain (See "Key to Prophecy" on the Former and Latter Rain). The word shattered in Hebrew is the word "*Narphats*" which means to disperse. In other words, the power of the holy people as witnesses will be poured out like rain during the "… Time of the End" (12:4). Christ spoke of this in Matthew. "But he who endures to the end shall be saved. And this gospel of the kingdom will be preached in all the world as a witness to all the nations, and then the end will come" (Matthew 24:13, 14).

THE FORMER RAIN AND THE LATTER RAIN

Key to Prophecy

There are many references to the former and latter rain in Scripture. Literally speaking, the "former rain" (early rain or first rain) occurred in the autumn of the year at the planting of the winter crops. This rain was required for the seed to sprout and get a good start before winter set in.

Figuratively the "former rain" is used to describe the outpouring of the Holy Spirit on the Day of Pentecost, which fulfilled the first part of the prophecy of Joel 2:23, and is referenced by Peter in Acts 2. The Holy Spirit was poured out like rain on the Day of Pentecost. The Holy Spirit is given to carry God's church through spiritual growth in preparation for the "latter rain".

Literally, the "latter rain" came in the spring when the rainy season was ending. It was needed for the grain to finish maturing before the harvest. It should be noted that without the "former rain" the "latter rain" was of no value.

The figurative reference to the "latter rain" fulfills the second half of Joel's prophecy in Joel 2:23 as Peter stated in Acts 2. "And it shall come to pass in the last days, says God, that I will pour out of My Spirit on all flesh; your sons and your daughters shall prophesy, your young men shall see visions, your old men shall dream dreams. And on My menservants and on My maidservants I will pour out My Spirit in those days" (Acts 2:17, 18).

The "… latter rain" (Joel 2:23) is the outpouring of the Holy Spirit during the "… Time of the End" (12:4), or "… last days" (Acts 2:17). Without the "… latter rain" (Joel 2:23), God's people, those that "… keep the commandments of God" (Revelation 14:12), will not grow to spiritual maturity and will not be able to stand and prevail through the final time of trouble. The "… latter rain" (Joel 2:23) prepares God's people to withstand the seven last plagues and will give them power to be witnesses and proclaim God's message. It ripens the grain for a massive harvest at the closing work of the gospel. It must be remembered; however, that unless the "… former rain" (Joel 2:23), the watering of the "baby seed" as on the Day of Pentecost occurs, the "… latter rain" (Joel 2:23) will yield no harvest.

12:7 GOD'S WITNESSES

Consider This

"But you shall receive power when the Holy Spirit has come upon you; and you shall be witnesses to Me in Jerusalem, and in all Judea and Samaria, and to the end of the earth" (Acts 1:8). The witness to the world will be that God's people are willing to follow His Word and keep His Sabbath as He has commanded.

The Loud Cry of Revelation 18, "… And he cried mightily with a strong voice, saying, Babylon the great is fallen, is fallen, and is become the habitation of devils, and the hold of every foul spirit, and a cage of every unclean and hateful bird. For all nations have drunk of the wine of the wrath of her fornication, and the kings of the earth have committed fornication with her, and the merchants of the earth are waxed rich through the abundance of her delicacies. And I heard another voice from heaven, saying, come out of her, My people, that ye be not partakers of her sins, and that ye receive not of her plagues" (Revelation 18:1–4), will be accompanied by the outpouring of the Holy Spirit (i.e. the latter rain).

"… When the power of the holy people has been completely shattered" (12:7) (i.e. Dispersed), meaning the power of the holy people as witnesses will be poured out like rain during the loud cry. For three and half years the last warning message will be given (1,260 literal days makes 3½ years—see Closer Look Daniel 12:11) and thousands will be converted just like on the Day of Pentecost in Acts 2:41. (See the "Key To Prophecy" on the Former and Latter Rain on the previous page for more information about this subject.)

12:9,10 The Time Element

9. And he said, "Go your way, Daniel, for the words are closed up and sealed till the time of the end. 10. "Many shall be purified, made white, and refined, but the wicked shall do wickedly; and none of the wicked shall understand, but the wise shall understand.

12:9,10 THE TIME ELEMENT

Closer Look

An understanding of this time element will be given to the righteous during the "… Time of the End" (12:9), or after 1798. Daniel did not understand the angel's use of the time elements. Always before, a day had represented a year. But in this case the angel used literal, and not prophetic time.

Always before when speaking of prophetic time Daniel used different Hebrew words such as:

• Daniel 7:25 in the original Hebrew is *"iddan"* or year.

• Daniel 8:14 is *"ereb-boqer"* or evening-morning.

However, when the angel tells Daniel, "But you, go your way till the end; for you shall rest, and will arise to your inheritance at the end of the days" (12:13), he uses the word *yowm* which is used in connection with literal days and not prophetic. This word is used by Daniel in chapter 1 in verses 12, 15, 18, concerning the ten day test he and his companions faced regarding their diet. In Daniel 6:7 it is used for the thirty days of royal decree. The word *yowm* is used in the book of Daniel only when referring to literal time. Therefore to be consistent we must conclude that the 1,260, the 1,290 and the 1,335 days of Daniel 12:11, 12 must be literal days.

12:11 The Daily Sacrifice

11. "And from the time that the daily sacrifice is taken away, and the abomination of desolation is set up, there shall be one thousand two hundred and ninety days.

12:11 THE DAILY SACRIFICE

Closer Look

Verse seven states that there will be "a time, times and a half time", or 1,260 days, until "… the power of the holy people has been completely shattered" (12:7). Using the time when the abomination of desolation starts, "… is set up" (12:11), as the beginning point, it would be 1,260 days until the power of the holy people has been completely shattered. With the abomination of desolation as the starting point and having the 1,260, 1,290, and 1,335 days; running concurrently, this brings us to events that are to take place in the last days. At the end of 1,260 days "… the daily sacrifice is taken away" (12:11).

What does "… the daily sacrifice is taken away" (12:11) mean? Which daily sacrifice is Michael talking about? First we need to establish, where is Michael? Michael is in Heaven (Revelation 12:7;

Acts 7:55, 56; Mark 14:62; Mark 16:19; Hebrews 1:3). Therefore, "… the daily sacrifice" (12:11), must refer to Christ's mediatoral work in the Heavenly Sanctuary. It is not referring back to the time when the Romans destroyed the temple and brought the EARTHLY daily sacrifices to an end because Michael is not on earth.

Michael is standing up, "At that time Michael shall stand up" (12:1), His work is finished. The intercession of Christ in man's behalf in the Heavenly Sanctuary has come to an end. He speaks the words described in Revelation 22:11, 12; "He who is unjust, let him be unjust still; he who is filthy, let him be filthy still; he who is righteous, let him be righteous still; he who is holy, let him be holy still. 'And behold, I am coming quickly, and My reward is with Me, to give to every one according to his work.'" The Scripture is clear (see Daniel 8:26; Revelation 22:10) that this will happen during the "... Time of the End" (12:9) —which began after 1798.

Daniel 12:10 states, "... but the wise shall understand" at the "... Time of the End" (12:10). Therefore, the beginning of these time periods, the 1260, 1290 and 1335 days of Daniel 12, or the "... wonders" (12:6), must take place after 1798. It is during this time that Christ's ministry in Heaven will come to an end.

At the beginning of the 1,260 days, the abomination of desolation will be set up. "... and the abomination of desolation is set up, there shall be one thousand two hundred and ninety days" (12:11). In Matthew 24:15, Jesus spoke of this as the setting up of a pagan idol in the temple area, setting aside the worship of God, the Creator of heaven and earth, and substituting in its place, the worship of a pagan god. Daniel 7:25 sheds light on what will happen in the last days. "He shall speak pompous words against the Most High, shall persecute the saints of the Most High, AND SHALL INTEND TO CHANGE TIMES AND LAW."

12:11 THE ABOMINATION OF DESOLATION

Consider This

We learned while studying chapter 7 that the power referred to here is the Papal system (Please reread the comments under 7:24–27). During the time of Papal Supremacy, the law of God was changed and the day of worship was set aside. In its place the day of the sun, (Sunday) was recognized as the day of worship. The sun was one of the pagan's greatest gods. In an effort to make Christianity appealing to the pagan, they replaced the Sabbath of the Lord with their idol sabbath - the day of the sun - which has it's origin in pagan belief and not in Scripture. The Roman power, at the time of the destruction of Jerusalem, committed the abominable act of setting up the pagan idol in the court of the temple, defying the God of Israel.

This act will be repeated again when the day comes that the Government enforces upon man the pagan sabbath (Sunday). This will be the abomination of desolation spoken of in Daniel 12:11 and will begin the 1,260 days. "Therefore, when you see the 'abomination of desolation', spoken of by Daniel the prophet, standing in the holy place (whoever reads, let him understand)" (Matthew 24:15).

"… When the power of the holy people has been completely shattered" (12:7), followers of God's commandments will be going through "… a time of trouble, such as never was since there was a nation, even to that time" (12:1). From the time the abomination of desolation starts, "… is set up" (12:11), there will be 1,260 days of trouble for those who keep the Sabbath.

12:11, 12 Blessed Is He Who Waits

12. "Blessed is he who waits, and comes to the one thousand three hundred and thirty-five days."

12:11, 12 BLESSED IS HE WHO WAITS

Consider This

The passing of a national Sunday law will bring about a time of persecution at the same time God's people are proclaiming the sacredness of God's Sabbath. At the end of three and half years (1,260 days), "At that time Michael will stand up" (12:1), and probation will close for mankind and the plagues mentioned in Revelation 15 will begin to fall.

Daniel states that the followers of God's commandments will be going through, "… a time of trouble, such as never was since there was a nation, even to that time" (12:1). As in the days of Mordecai and Esther, "… let a decree be written that they be destroyed" (Esther 3:9), a death decree will be passed upon all those who do not worship the beast. "He was granted power to give breath to the image of the beast [Sunday enforcement], that the image of the beast should both speak and cause as many as would not worship the image of the beast to be killed" (Revelation 13:15.) This death decree, which is part of the abomination of desolation, will come at the end of the 1,290 days. In faith, the righteous will wait 45 days which brings them to the end of 1,335 days. "Blessed is he who waits, and comes to the one thousand three hundred and thirty-five days" (12:12). At this time, the saints will be delivered. Since these events are still future, and we do not know when Christ's ministry in the heavenly sanctuary will come to an end, "… Michael shall stand up" (12:1), we cannot know the day or the hour of the Lord's coming.

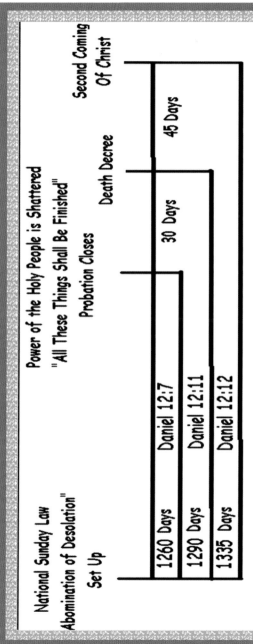

Daniel 12:7: Then I heard the man clothed in linen, who was above the waters of the river, when he held up his right hand and his left hand to heaven, and swore by Him who lives forever, that it shall be for a time, times and half a time; and when the power of the holy people has been completely shattered, all these things shall be finished.

Daniel 12:11: "And from the time that the daily sacrifice is taken away, and the abomination of desolation is set up, there shall be one thousand two hundred and ninety days.

Daniel 12:12: "Blessed is he who waits, and comes to the one thousand three hundred and thirty-five days.

Faith Builders

Last Faith Builder

12:13 Faith's Anchor

There are situations in the life of Daniel which give us indications of how he built his faith. Hebrews 11:6 says, "Without faith you cannot please God". The six examples in this book of how he built his faith are needed in today's hectic society.

Faith is believing in what God has done. Daniel could see clearly how God had led his life in the past. His prayers had been answered; some of the prophecies had already been fulfilled. God's Word was true; he had a solid foundation upon which to build his faith. Faith is also believing in what God can do. Daniel was praying and working for the restoration of the Jewish people. Cyrus had already made a decree letting the children of Israel go back to Jerusalem. There were difficulties with the Samaritans but the Lord had assured Daniel He was working in their behalf. Faith is believing in what God is going to do. Now Daniel could rest in the Lord, knowing the people of God would be cared for, and all would rejoice together at the resurrection.

12:13 Rest Daniel

13. "But you, go your way till the end; for you shall rest, and will arise to your inheritance at the end of the days."

12:13 REST DANIEL

Closer Look

Daniel lived a wonderful life. He served as prime-minister of two countries. But most importantly, he had a close relationship with his Lord. Now the time had come for him to rest. He simply closed his eyes in the sleep of death, and will rest until the end of days (meaning the 1,335 days). It will have seemed but a moment when he will awake at the end of time to see his Savior and receive his inheritance.

158

Notes

Notes